Releasing Bonds from the Courts of Heaven

Uncovering Bonds & Establishing Bonds

Second Edition

Volume 1 of the Bonds & Trust Series

By

Dr. Ron M. Horner

Releasing Bonds from the Courts of Heaven

Uncovering Bonds & Establishing Bonds

Second Edition

Volume 1 of the Bonds & Trust Series

By

Dr. Ron M. Horner

LifeSpring International Ministries
PO Box 5847
Pinehurst, North Carolina 28374
www.RonHorner.com

Releasing Bonds from the Courts of Heaven
Uncovering Bonds & Establishing Bonds
Second Edition

Copyright © 2023 Dr. Ron M. Horner

Scripture is taken from the New King James Version®. Copyright © 1982 by Thomas Nelson. Used by permission. All rights reserved. (Unless otherwise noted.)

Scripture quotations marked (KJV) are from the King James Version of the Bible.

Any trademarks mentioned are the property of their respective owners.

All rights reserved. This book is protected by the copyright laws of the United States of America. This book may not be copied or reprinted for commercial gain or profit. The use of short quotations or occasional page copying for personal, or group study is permitted and encouraged. Permission will be granted upon request.

Requests for bulk sales discounts, editorial permissions, or other information should be addressed to:

LifeSpring Publishing
PO Box 5847
Pinehurst, NC 28374 USA

Additional copies available at www.courtsofheaven.net

ISBN 13 TP: 978-1-953684-26-4
ISBN 13 eBook: 978-1-953684-27-1

Cover by David Munoz
(davidmunozart.com)

Second Edition: August 2023

10 9 8 7 6 5 4 3 2 1 0

Printed in the United States of America

Table of Contents

Acknowledgments i
Preface iii
Chapter 1 It's Class Time 1
Chapter 2 Types of Bonds 5
Chapter 3 Working with the Faith of Another 25
Chapter 4 Dealing with the Bond of Iniquity 37
Chapter 5 Spiritual Booby Traps 53
Chapter 6 Back in the Classroom 61
Chapter 7 Understanding the Registry 67
Chapter 8 Sample Writs 75
Chapter 9 Writ of Severance 87
Chapter 10 Various Bonds 93
        Ungodly Bonds 93
        Godly Bonds 95
Chapter 11 Working with Bond Registry Angels 101
Chapter 12 Bonds in Governmental Intercession 109
Chapter 13 Sources of Ungodly Bonds 121
Chapter 14 Trading on Ungodly Bonds 133
Chapter 15 Two New Bonds 141
Chapter 16 Q & A Time 145

Chapter 17 Return to Sender 157
Chapter 18 Blessings vs. Bonds 169
Chapter 19 Surety Bonds 181
Chapter 20 Conclusion.. 187
Appendix A... 191
Bonds Listing... 191
    Godly 191
    Ungodly Bonds... 203
Works Cited 213
Description 215
About the Author 217
Other Books by Dr. Ron M. Horner............................. 219

Acknowledgments

In this edition *Releasing Bonds from the Courts of Heaven*, Stephanie Shearin has come alongside to assist in engagements with Heaven for revelation. I honor and thank her for her humble service to the King. You are deeply appreciated.

Preface

Having released the original book *(Releasing Bonds from the Courts of Heaven)* in 2020, nearly two years to the day, Heaven downloaded a batch of new materials that we were instructed to include in the updated book, which is now the first in a series on Bonds and Trusts. This new understanding, coupled with an expanded knowledge of spiritual bonds, will significantly enhance the freedom people gain who receive and activate this revelation in their lives.

Due to the volume of material, we have divided this material into two books. This book is primarily material from the Releasing Bonds book, with additional insights and testimonies. The second volume will cover the subject of Trusts and Consequential Liens.

Our ministry has been transformed through understanding Godly bonds and knowing how to remove ungodly bonds. We still don't understand all we would like to about bonds, but we do know they have a particular level of spiritual strength in peoples' lives. That can be good or bad, depending on the type of bond.

Knowing what is on one's Bond Registry is often very beneficial in unraveling the bondages that hold people. We have been surprised to read the variety of bonds and how the counsels of hell are sometimes scraping the bottom of the barrel trying to get something negative placed on someone's life.

We have learned that we can sometimes ascertain the source of bonds placed on us. That can be good information to know. We have also learned of some that enable us not to be pestered by workers of darkness who seem to have nothing else to do.

The newest understanding regards Godly and ungodly trusts. The Father has enacted a series of trusts on our behalf, which our enemy has attempted to circumvent. A form of a simple trust is a legal instrument designed to restrict access to an inheritance. Ungodly trusts created from the courts of hell do precisely that. They restrict access to our inheritance. The book *Dealing with Trusts & Consequential Liens in the Courts of Heaven*[1] discusses an aspect of that. There are also trusts that offer specific benefits only available to some. The issue of trusts is an entirely new concept to us, but one that will result in tremendous freedom for those whose lives have been a constant storm where they have not been able to gain freedom.

Freedom *IS* available! You are about to see it manifest in your life. Finding out where we are in relation to

---

[1] LifeSpring Publishing, 2022.

various aspects of trust in our lives is also crucial. We will explain that in the coming chapters and subsequent books in this series.

We were given a simple outline that will be explained later in the book, but it will help you understand the power of the revelation we have received.

The original content of this book (that about bonds) will remain largely the same. A step-by-step for bonds is in Chapter 8. We will make insertions from time to time based on new understandings and concepts gained from Heaven, but you will see that beginning in Chapter 11, we introduce additional concepts relating to bonds in this book. If you are new to this concept, it will be life changing. If you have already read the first edition of Releasing Bonds, you are in for an exciting ride due to the new revelation unveiled about bonds and the power thereof. Enjoy!

———·———

Chapter 1
It's Class Time

As my seer and I stepped into the realms of Heaven, we went to the Help Desk to inquire where we needed to go for information concerning bonds. An angel began to speak to us on the subject, but we sensed we were only scratching the surface of what we needed to know.

According to the Oxford Dictionary, a bond is an agreement with legal force. (Oxford Dictionary: Bond). A secondary definition is that a bond is a deed by which a person is committed to pay another. Our heavenly tutor would vastly broaden this definition for us in the next few moments.

Our first question involved where we go to obtain a bond, and we were instructed that it depended upon the type of bond. She did not elaborate on that point but went on to describe different existing bonds. Bonds bring clarity and agreement to people and situations.

She described a bit about Financial Bonds that come out of the realms of Heaven. They attach something from the realms of Heaven to others on the earth. It *increases the likelihood of the recipient receiving what the requestor attached or requested of the realms of Heaven.* In the case of a financial bond, we remember Philippians 4:19:

And my God shall supply all your need according to His riches in glory by Christ Jesus.

For example, "Father, I request on behalf of _____, a bond of Philippians 4:19, in Jesus' name."

Heaven has unlimited resources to benefit the sons of men, yet we have not learned well how to get those resources from the realms of Heaven into the earth. This understanding of bonds is a tool to help bring that about.

The angel assisting us at this point gave the example of a school that needed supplies. She described that a bond from a believer can be requested so that an attachment is made on that believer's faith from the realms of Heaven to benefit the school. It is impacted by one's faith. The greater the faith you have for a thing, the stronger the attached bond will be.

Great faith equates to a stronger attached bond.

She described how a bond ties two things together.

A bond ties two things together.

In the case of a financial bond, it ties the resources of Heaven to the need upon the earth (i.e., the school supplies) via the faith of a third-party who is releasing faith on behalf of those in need and placing a spiritual demand upon the resources of Heaven to manifest in the earth.

We asked, "Can you explain how this would feel to the recipient?"

She told us, "A bond is usually given where there is strong enforcement of a request that ties two things together. It links two parties with a legal agreement."

The Classroom

At this point, we needed more detailed instructions. We respectfully asked if a tutor could teach us about bonds and how to utilize them. We pointed out that we were requesting information on bonds from a legal standpoint.

We were directed to a classroom in the Courts of Heaven. As we entered, we saw computer screens on desks and a tutor ready to teach us. This tutor was not an angel but one of the Men in White Linen. He began teaching us about bonds. We were able to have an interchange for about an hour. We will be unveiling what was revealed to us in the coming pages.

Categories of Bonds

Two categories of bonds exist, we were told: legal & non-legal (emotional bonds). However, not all emotional bonds are illegal, as we will discover later.

Legal bonds create a legal bond of the spirit. It achieves the effect of a net where the recipient's need is the net that is enabled to catch the resources of Heaven as they are released to the earth. A bond carries things between two parties. It helps ease the burden of one party through the other party's desire. It creates an arrangement through which the angelic can move and route resources in certain directions. These are the positive ways to utilize a bond in the realm of Heaven, we were told.

Our tutor continued unveiling details about bonds that we knew would be life changing. We were in awe of the experience we were having and the depth of the information we were receiving. Next, he began unveiling the various types of bonds and how to implement them. Let's discover this together!

_____ · _____

Chapter 2
Types of Bonds

We sat in a classroom as our instructor began unveiling a few of the many types of bonds available. Although I had been working in the Courts of Heaven for several years, these understandings were just now being released to us. We knew this information was massively significant for this time. We are about to share precisely as it was shared with us. We would have to unpack the specifics of this revelation later. The first type of bond to be unveiled in this segment was the Clarity Bond.

Clarity Bond

A release of the functionality of clarity, vision, and/or expectation happens with this bond. It is attached to a record and an account. Clarity is a substance of Heaven and can be released from Heaven.

We know from Hebrews 11:1[2] that faith is a substance, and we were now shown that many more things are substances than we had previously considered. As a bond is a legal matter from Heaven, it ensures that angelic hosts can affect the change on the earth. (It backs them up.)

A Clarity Bond can be requested in the courts by anyone for someone else, and upon being granted, it releases to the other party a degree of clarity that is otherwise unlikely to be obtained.

---

*An example of a clarity bond
is how it grants wisdom
for actualizing unknown things.*

I asked our tutor, "Do we need a Clarity Bond for what we are doing now?" He replied that it was useful but not required. Because I was pressed for time (it was a few minutes after five in the afternoon, and I had a class to teach at seven—and this was going to be the subject), I opted out of the Bond of Clarity at that time. I intended to return later to find out how one is obtained.

---

[2] Hebrews 11:1 "Now faith is the substance of things hoped for, the evidence of things not seen."

Writ of Release

A Writ of Release effectuates a release of resources that another party can encounter but *is based on the faith of the initiating party*. All the bonds we were to discover were based seemingly on the one with stronger faith.

> *A Writ of Release effectuates a release of resources that another party can encounter but is based on the faith of the initiating party.*

The purpose of obtaining a bond is to release the resources of Heaven for someone whose faith was weaker.

Emotional Bonds

Emotional bonds can be requested by one party to another, such as in the case of a married couple. It utilizes the faith of one toward another. It links the two. It operates somewhat like an enabling. (In case your mind tells you that being an enabler is a negative thing, we were told at that point that in Heaven it is not a negative thing.) It enables the recipient to enjoy the relationship with the other party.

Maternal Bonds

Another type of positive emotional bond can be between a mother and her children. It employs the emotional avenue to release an enjoyment of "what should be" based on the faith of the initiating party. God designed mothers to have a special bond with their children. It initiates during the pregnancy and upon delivery of the baby, the first few moments are crucial to the bonding of the parents to the child. Sometimes this cannot happen, so it needs to be reinforced later, and obtaining a Maternal Bond can help establish what God originally intended for that mother and child.

Often marriages go through rough spots, and the couples become distant. If your marriage needs some help, ask someone *with a stronger marriage* to request in the courts a Bond of Unity regarding your marriage. Sometimes a Bond of Clarity is helpful to refocus one or both parties on their love for each other.

We paused to ask, "Can you tell us how this is used? In the Father's Kingdom, is a bond used to protect oneself or as a weapon against the enemy? When would you use one?"

Using the Emotional Bond

In the case of the emotional bond, it is used weapon-like, as it is off-putting to the enemy and can be seen in the spirit. It may not be apparent initially in the natural arena, but it is very evident in the spirit realm. It links a more robust faith to a weaker faith. It helps effectuate an ability to believe. It is from one party to another.

So that is how it releases resources as well. A strong believer initiating a bond of a substance (of Heaven's resources) to another person releases that Heavenly substance through their faith for the resources of the Kingdom (whatever the need is) for the benefit of the weaker in faith. Whenever a bond is issued from the resources of Heaven, whether it is love between a husband and wife, love of the brethren, or affection between parents and children, it enables the weaker party to receive from the storehouses of Heaven based on the initiating party's request. It is likened to *standing in the gap*.

Which Court?

We then asked where we go in the Courts of Heaven to request a bond like this. We were told, the Court of Titles & Deeds. As we pondered this, more revelation came. *It is the moving of property from one place to another by means of the spirit realm.* All the bonds we were taught about were to be requested in the Court of Titles and Deeds. Revelation began to pour forth concerning the early church and how a bond was used to transfer the resources of Heaven to the church on the earth.

Now all who believed were together, and had all things in common, [45] and sold their possessions and goods, and divided them among all, as anyone had need. [46] So continuing daily with one accord in the temple, and breaking bread from house to house, they ate their food with gladness and simplicity of heart, [47] praising God and having favor with all the people. And the Lord added to the church daily those who were being saved. (Acts 2:44-47)

Unity Bond

A Unity Bond can be obtained when the leaders of a body (and those in agreement with the leadership) request a Unity Bond on behalf of the larger body. The leader of the body would initiate the Bond of Unity by obtaining a Writ of Unity (Unity Bond) for the benefit of the body in the Court of Titles and Deeds. A writ is a formal written order. In this case, a writ is attached to a bond, defining specific aspects of the overall bond.

We asked the question, "Do both parties have to be in agreement for the bond?"

Our tutor answered, "They have to agree with the Holy Spirit (the 3rd party). Because it is a heavenly legal matter, the leadership can choose to establish this bond in the court and request that it be established." It is this agreement with the Holy Spirit that allowed the bond to have maximum impact in the life of the church. The leader can establish it in the courts for the other parties.

Our tutor pointed out that the phrase "holding all things together as one"[3] is vital for the language to communicate what was done in the spirit. It was linked to the manifestation of the request made in the spirit. It was very supernatural. It was based on the leadership's faith desiring that none in the body should go without. However, the agreement of the recipients with the leadership and Holy Spirit, as Holy Spirit acted upon them caused the bond to manifest on the earth. It manifested so thoroughly that it placed the church in the position to significantly influence the world over the next few years. This bond is requested in the Court of Titles and Deeds, where you ask the court to release a Unity Bond, Emotion Bond, Financial Bond, or whatever type of bond you are requesting.

To obtain one of these bonds is quite simple, and we will detail that shortly because you are simply requesting the Court to release the bond on behalf of the other party. Anyone may ask for the release of the various bonds for another person or a group.

---

[3] Acts 2:44

> *It is a legal matter from Heaven ensuring that angelic hosts have the backup required, allowing for the release of the manifestation of whatever the request was for.*

It backs up the angels to ensure that the deed happens.

Safety Bond

Paul had obtained a Safety Bond regarding the sinking of all the passengers on the ship on which he was a passenger. The bond was the paperwork necessary to ensure the passengers' safety. Acts 27 describes the story. Paul, via communication with an angel, requested a "Writ of Release for the Safety of All on the Boat." This writ ensured that it happened due to Paul's request in the Courts.

> *The bond is the overall legal paperwork. The writ contains the specifics of the bond.*

The bond is actualized through the writ. We know from the story in Acts that Paul's courtroom work resulted in no loss of life for those on the ship.

Once the tutor described the backstory to Acts 27, it was clear that a Safety Bond had been issued. Other instances in the Bible detail similar things. In Exodus 14, we read the story of the children of Israel coming to the Red Sea while under the leadership of Moses. He essentially obtained a Writ of Safety for the Children of Israel and a Writ of Deliverance from the Egyptians. Moses had faith, whereas the children of Israel had none.

Financial Bond

A Financial Bond releases resources of Heaven on behalf of another. We discussed this in chapter one, so a repeat unnecessary now.

Requisitions vs. Bonds

A bond is always for another party's benefit, *not the benefit of the one making the request,* whereas *a requisition may benefit the one making the request.* A bond utilizes the stronger faith of one believer (one with more maturity, understanding, or unction) for another person. It helps all grow up in Christ by not requiring the less knowledgeable to gain resources of Heaven, whether finances, safety, emotional comfort, or other things. *Their faith is jump-started.* The angels are more intentional about helping the receiver obtain the benefits of the bond.

> *A bond is a separate legal force stronger than a regular petition or request.*

We inquired, "Does this need to be a formal request in the courts, or does it happen a lot because we are following Holy Spirit and simply asking or believing for certain things?"

Our tutor replied, "It is a separate thing because it is much stronger in its legal force—*it is legally backed up when we have a Writ of Release.*" It can help jump-start the faith of a weaker believer.

At this point, he began to speak to the seer about a family situation regarding her daughter. She was told she could go to the Court of Titles and Deeds and request a bond—a Writ of Release of Faith for her daughter to hold on to the fact that she will be pregnant.[4] *This bond utilizes the seer's faith as a conduit for her faith but is done in the spirit through the legal acquisition of the bond.* Her daughter would then be undergirded in her faith for what was requested in the bond. Because the angels have the paperwork, they will be more intentional in seeing that she walks in this measure of faith. There seems to be *extra assistance given* to the daughter to stay in faith. They will war in battles to victory if needed, and if

---

[4] The seer became a grandmother in 2021.

necessary, they will provide general comfort and assistance in heart and mind to believe.

Bond of Perfection

The phrase Bond of Perfection (or Maturity) is found in Colossians 3:14 where we read:

> *But above all these things put on love, which is the bond of perfection.*

We asked if the Bond of Perfection was a way to jump-start the faith of the Colossian believers.

Paul's faith for them to be grown up quickly was what he initiated in the legal realm of Heaven by this bond. Paul's bond aided their faith so they would not stumble as much. If you read the letter to the Colossians (particularly using The Passion Translation), you can see how Paul was commending the Colossians for their spiritual growth. He essentially says that they had learned to receive directly from Heaven the things he would have taught them when he came to visit them. Because they had excelled in that manner, he could proceed to teach them other things. They had caught Paul's heart and desire to live out of the realms of Heaven and had successfully learned to do so.

Bond of Peace

Another bond mentioned in Paul's writing is the Bond of Peace.

> *...endeavoring to keep the <u>unity of the Spirit</u> in the bond of peace. (Ephesians 4:3) [Emphasis added]*

We were instructed that this bond was a Clarity Bond for Unity. *A guarantee of like-mindedness* was released through that bond.

The churches of Ephesus were able to walk in extraordinary unity because of this bond.

Why the Court of Titles and Deeds?

Because the resources are in Heaven, and this is affecting a transfer of resources from one place to another—from one owner to another, it would be handled in the Court of Titles and Deeds. *It's like a lease agreement.* It is a lease on the resources. It is not an "ownership" issue per se. It is more of a lease arrangement where the resources of Heaven are brought into the earth.

We then asked if we could share this with our Tuesday Night LifeSpring Mentoring Group. We were given a release, and at that point, were handed a scroll. We were also given some instructions to share, which I'll cover in the Conclusion at the end of the book.

As we discussed some of the impact of these Writs, we began to understand more fully how one could have more faith, more clarity, or more strength for a thing through them.

When the recipient agrees *with the Holy Spirit concerning the writ being released, its impact can be even stronger.*

We could apply this to creativity. We were told finances were a common application, as were safety, positive emotions such as more confidence—specifically someone's spiritual confidence, and so on.

How Would This Help Someone Struggling With Fear?

Fear is the lack of confidence in love and love's ability. It agrees with the wrong thing. It is faith for the wrong thing.

Examples:

- Writ of Release for an Undergirding
- Writ of Release for a Sense of Not Being Alone

These examples seem related to why someone would be afraid in the first place. They are kept in place through a believed lie.

A benefit of a bond is Heaven trading on Heaven's bounty, the goodness of God, and the knowledge of the resources that are in Heaven on behalf of another.

This can be used where we see a lack in someone's life. Wisdom is something you could request a Writ of Release for.

A Bond of Wisdom
is a Writ of Release for Wisdom

If any of you lacks wisdom, let him ask of God, who gives to all liberally and without reproach, and it will be given to him. James 1:5

Does the Body of Christ Use This?

We asked, "Does the Body of Christ use this very much?"

Our instructor answered us, "No. They use a lesser form or format of request, and is what they mean when they say, 'I bless you!' or 'I bless you to have a good day!'" Whereas that may be a good sentiment, the release of a bond for a day full of blessings would be a much stronger legal matter.

Churches are in great need of doing this. They need leaders of one body to request the release of a bond on behalf of a receiving body. The leaders need to do this corporately. The 'sharing of all things as one had need' recorded in the book of Acts was a testimony of the power of a corporate bond.

But now God has set the members, each one of them, in the body just as He pleased. [19] And if they were all one member, where would the body be? [20] But now indeed there are many members, yet one body. [21] And the eye cannot say to the hand, 'I have no need of you'; nor again the head to the feet, 'I have no need of you.' [22] No, much rather, those members of the body which seem to be weaker are necessary. [23] And those members of the body which we think to be less honorable, on these we bestow greater honor; and our unpresentable parts have greater modesty, [24] but our presentable parts have no need. But God composed the body, having given greater honor to that part which lacks it, [25] that there should be no schism in the body, but that the members should have the same care for one another. [26] And if one member suffers, all the members suffer with it; or if one member is honored, all the members rejoice with it. [27] Now you are the Body of Christ, and members individually. [28] And God has appointed these in the church: first apostles, second prophets, third teachers, after that, miracles, then gifts of healings, helps, administrations, varieties of tongues. (1 Corinthians 12:18-28)

The offices listed in verse 28 are responsible for releasing these bonds on behalf of the believers.

The leaders are to be releasing bonds on behalf of the people.

It is a responsibility of the Ascension Gift Ministries of Ephesians 4.

> *And He Himself gave some to be apostles, some prophets, some evangelists, and some pastors and teachers, ^{12} for the equipping of the saints for the work of ministry, for the edifying of the Body of Christ, ^{13} till we all come to the unity of the faith [via a Unity Bond] and of the knowledge of the Son of God [via a Clarity Bond], to a perfect man [via a Bond of Maturity], to the measure of the stature of the fullness of Christ. (Ephesians 4:11-13) [Emphasis mine]*

If the leaders would release bonds on behalf of the people, the people would be growing up into Christ Jesus at an accelerated rate.

Our tutor began showing how the lack of using this harms the church. When you have a leader, who is not obtaining bonds on behalf of his church, the church suffers needlessly.

The church is not receiving the release because the leaders are not releasing bonds.

> *All are experiencing lack
> when they don't have to.*

This is a result of the church going through its ups and downs (which it would not have to experience so much if the bonds were being released effectively).

When a leader utilizes the spirit of control and manipulation instead of leading out of Heaven's resources and using the members' natural lack to control them so they will follow that leader, the leader is wrong. To do that is wrong.

> *Church leaders should be releasing
> the resources of Heaven to them,
> ensuring their growth and expansion
> in the things of God.*

A leader who is not doing that is not effectively dealing with issues of control, manipulation, spirits of Jezebel, and spirits of wickedness.

Testimonies

From LR:

I want to share an experience I had after our mentoring call on Tuesday, January 14. DE. called me and asked if I would pray for a bond for her reading. She has had difficulty lately with being able to maintain focus when she tries to read. She then would ask for a bond for me for improvement in my memory, which I have had trouble with for a while.

When I sat down to pray about this, I wasn't quite sure how to approach the subject of a bond because I had not listened to the replay of the [Mentoring] session yet. I had made notes on all the slides but didn't feel confident yet. As I waited, I felt in my knower that there was a lien against her reading. I went to Titles and Deeds and asked that this lien be marked satisfied and any false titles against her reading be removed.

As I was praying about this, I realized that I had unconsciously made a vow regarding my memory. Now I can see that the Lord has been reminding me of this for some time now, but it just didn't click with me. I went to the Mercy Court and repented of making this vow and asked that it be put under the Blood of Jesus and that all ramifications of that vow be removed. Then I went back to Titles and Deeds and asked that any lien against my memory be marked satisfied and any false titles be removed, and ownership changed back to Jesus.

I just watched the replay and now have a much better understanding of the bonds so now will go back and ask for the appropriate bonds for DE. Thank you for this timely information.

This started an exchange on Facebook:

DE: Thank you LR for your love in securing my bond. I spent time reading last night Ron's Unlocking Spiritual Seeing. I told my soul to rest and listen to what I was reading. After a few times of that, I successfully read out loud for an hour. I am grateful for this revelation. Really opens a deeper understanding of the Love of our Lord for us. His Glory. I do honor and bless you all. And I have great expectation for a new level of seeing.

Me to LR: I have requested a Bond of Clarity regarding your spiritual sight for you. Happy seeing!

LR to me: Thank you Ron. I receive it in Jesus' Name! I already see change! Praise Father! Son and Holy Spirit! All honor and glory to Him!

——— · ———

Releasing GODLY bonds is the gift that keeps on giving. I just started doing it last week and I saw the fruit but this AM, I did it and it was like bam bam bam. I am so excited! EVERYONE GETS BLESSINGS, MIRACLES, AND SIGNS AND WONDERS!!

WHOO HOOO!!

Thank you so much! I love this, and it's such a blessing. So fun to see it come to fruition.

Thank you for obeying FATHER with this HEAVEN revelation! GO Courts of Heaven!

– MG

———·———

Chapter 3

Working with the Faith of Another

Scripture tells us that God has given every man a measure of faith. That measure of faith,[5] even as small as a grain of a mustard seed,[6] is powerful enough to accomplish any need.

In Mark 11:22, Jesus instructs us to "have the faith OF God (emphasis mine). Instead of relying upon mankind for the use of any person's faith, in and of itself, God himself provided for us His faith, so when we exercise what we have referred to as our faith, we are actually exercising His faith. All of us would agree that God's faith is probably more potent than our personal faith.

We build our faith by constant use. When we exercise faith toward the fulfillment of a desire, and we see the desire manifested in our 3-D world, it builds our faith to

---

[5] Romans 12:3

[6] Matthew 17:20

believe on a greater level than we previously have experienced, and so it should be that way.

You may have received a tricycle to ride when you were a small child. As a baby, you developed the ability to sit upright; then, you weren't satisfied with that because you saw something across the room that you wanted to explore, so you began propelling yourself toward the desired object. Eventually, you progressed to crawling and not just scooting yourself across the floor. Then, you weren't satisfied with that, so you began to try to stand, and eventually, the big day came when you stood up, and propelled yourself forward. Awkwardly at first, you finally mastered walking.

Again, you weren't satisfied just walking; you had to climb. You saw other children running, and so you began to try that and began running. You fell a few times, but you wouldn't be deterred. You were going to run!

Then you saw kids older than you going faster on these things with wheels. Maybe you received one of these contraptions for Christmas or your birthday, and you began to learn to master this 3-wheeled device. You played and rode on your tricycle, but not being satisfied with that, you progressed to riding a bicycle. Now you could go really fast!

Every step in this evolution of ability and confidence was an exercise of faith by you and by others toward you that you could do each of these things. You were building faith!

Faith is designed to be exercised. Years ago, I shattered my left wrist in a work accident. I had to have a couple of surgeries to repair all the damage, and as a result, my hand and wrist were immobilized for several weeks. It only took a few days before the muscles in my arm began to atrophy and get weaker. The muscle tone decreased, and the muscles became flabby.

Once out of the stabilizer as my bones healed, I spent several weeks of physical therapy regaining strength in my arm and rebuilding the ability to perform simple tasks. At first, I would not drink from a glass because it was too likely that the weight of the drink in the glass would prove too much for my weakened hand. I had to progress in building my strength. Some abilities returned rather quickly, while others took months to return. The strength of my left hand and arm was greatly diminished from my right hand and arm. Yet, through exercise, eventually, I could do most things I had once done with my left hand and arm.

The writer of Hebrews spoke of this in Hebrews 5:14:

*But solid food belongs to those who are of full age, that is, those who **by reason of use** have their senses exercised to discern both good and evil.*

By reason of use, by practicing and developing one's skills, a person is able to get better and better.

The Faith of Another

Sometimes you need someone to join you in an exercise of faith for something. For instance, you need a certain amount of money for a situation. You have successfully seen God provide for you in the past for certain amounts, but the most you may have experienced supernatural provision for was $5,000. However, in this situation, you need a much larger sum, several times larger. Your faith is not exercised to that degree—yet.

You have a friend, however, that has seen God provide much larger sums of money. What you need to do, is get them to join their faith with yours. You may not "have the faith" to believe for $100,000, but maybe they do.

Jesus gave us a promise in Matthew 18:19-20 when he said,

> *Again, assuredly I am saying to you, If **two of you upon the earth are in agreement**, concerning every matter of which they ask that something be given it shall become theirs from the presence of my Father who is in heaven. For where there are two or three who have been joined together into my Name with the result that **I am the common object of their faith**, there I am in their midst. (Wuest) [Emphasis added]*

We have a promise. We don't need one hundred people to agree with us; we only need one. Jesus made it extremely simple. If you can find two or three to agree with you, that is even better.

In Old Testament times, when two parties agreed on something, sometimes they would cut covenant with one another to symbolize their agreement. At other times they simply shook hands and pledged their agreement. They created legally binding paperwork by those pledges, the nature of which would stand until the end result of that pledge was fulfilled. They came into agreement and did not come out of agreement simply because it became inconvenient.

In our culture, we are quick to break agreements. My father taught me a valuable lesson: his word was his bond. If he told you he would do something, you could take it to the bank. It was as good as accomplished. Regarding the act of coming into agreement, we need to stay in agreement for the whole term. Don't be moved by circumstances.

Years ago, we needed to replace one of our vehicles. We did not have much money to purchase another. Still, I determined what I wanted in a replacement vehicle, researched and knew the approximate replacement cost. I asked a friend that I had confidence in to agree with me for the amount of money to come into my hands to make the purchase. He simply said to me, "I am in agreement with you."

Less than three weeks later, the funds had come from various sources, and we were driving that new car. We had come into agreement and not come out.

When it comes to bonds...

---

*The greater the faith
of the one requesting the bond,
the greater the likelihood
of its manifestation in the life
of the recipient of that bond.*

When someone requests a bond on your behalf, be sure to come into agreement with that person to fulfill that bond. Don't simply thank them. Join what faith you do possess with their faith.

---

*Joining your faith with the faith
of the requestor multiplies
the likelihood of fulfillment.*

You may not have had sufficient faith for a certain thing, but that does not mean they did not have faith for it.

---

*The fact that you will agree with them
and join your faith with theirs
will even further strengthen their
faith which will further strengthen
your faith, creating a cycle of faith.*

That cycle of faith will energize and active angels, not just angels of the bond registry angels, but also your angels and the angels of the requestor of the bonds. This angelic activity will ensure that the thing requested comes into your life. It will even increase the likelihood of even more rapid deployment of the resources of Heaven on your behalf.

When releasing bonds, be sure to include the Writ of Release of specifics related to that bond.

> *It is in the Writ of Release that the finalizing of the bond occurs.*

The Writ of Release lists the specifics of the bond.

For instance, you may request a bond of peace for someone, but what kind of peace? What are the specifics of the bond? The Writ of Release may look like this:

Father, I request a Bond of Peace for the person reading this book with a Writ of Release for a sweeping over their life with the sweet presence of Heaven, a renewed awareness of the activity of angels, and the clarity to sense this angelic activity to produce an energizing and bolstering of their faith.

If you, at this moment, will agree with this bond request, you will release the resources of Heaven to bring this into your life. Simply say, "I am in agreement with Dr. Horner for this bond and the subsequent Writ of Release."

You will be amazed at how God shows up in your life when you learn to activate the Law of Agreement of Matthew 18:19-20.

The Faith of Heaven

Some of us have been mistakenly taught that we won't need faith when we get to Heaven. Heaven has informed us that you will always exercise faith to some degree, even after you pass from this life to the next.

Scripture tells us that some things will pass away, such as knowledge (specifically the reliance on human-based knowledge), tongues, and prophecy. The latter two won't be needed because our means of communication may be more telekinetic than verbal.

Let me ask, "Do you think Moses had faith for provision?"

Of course, he did. Over the course of nearly 40 years, He had seen God provide daily for millions of people. He witnessed water coming from a rock. He saw the army of Pharaoh annihilated in a matter of moments as the waters of the Red Sea came crashing in upon them after having parted at the instruction of Moses a short time before.

When Moses died, did his faith die with him? No. He still has it to operate from. After teaching on bonds during our mentoring group, a friend texted me a question. He asked, "Can we ask people in Heaven to attach their faith to the bond process?"

I responded that I had never thought about it, so I recommended he ask Heaven. He did, and Heaven's reply was, "We've been waiting for you to figure that out."

That opens a whole new arena of possibilities, doesn't it?

In Hebrews 11, we read about various patriarchs and how faith impacted their lives. Now, that is great information to read, but we have kept it limited to life on this side of the veil. Moses knew a great deal about the exercise of faith for daily provision. He knew how to get one's light bill paid if you understand what I am saying!

It would not be a struggle for him to believe for the provision to replace your old prayer car. A prayer car is one that you pray it will start, pray it will keep going, and pray it will stop when you need it too! Some of you may be driving one of those now.

The wonderful thing is you don't have to be embarrassed by your request with anyone in Heaven. Remember, Moses, Noah, Abraham, and all the others listed are not dead, they have simply changed locations to a different realm or dimension.

Enoch had faith for transrelocation and translocation. Do you think he would join his faith with yours. What if you were to ask him to agree with you for you to experience translocation or transrelocation? What if?

Noah obeyed God's instruction, resulting in the preservation of his and his family's lives as the progenitors of humanity on earth. Would he add his faith to yours to see your family preserved?

Abraham obeyed by going to a new location. Do you suppose he would attach his faith to yours for you to have the courage to make a move?

The list goes on with various men and women exercising faith while on the earth and being willing to join their faith with yours and see Heaven's resources released into the earth. We have just scratched the surface tapping into the resource of the faith of the saints who have gone before us. Their faith did not die! It lives on! Let us avail ourselves of it.

In fact, Hebrews 11:13 records:

These all died in faith, not having received the promises, but having seen them afar off were assured of them, embraced them and confessed that they were strangers and pilgrims on the earth.

They died IN faith, but scripture does not say their faith died. It is just as alive and active as ever and can be utilized on your behalf.

How to Put This to Use

Suppose you want someone to come alongside you and strengthen your faith—bring it to a whole new level by coming into agreement with you. Step into Heaven, request to meet with the saint you sense could join you in faith, and ask if they would join their faith with yours for the thing you need, or if asking for a bond for someone, would they join their faith with yours on behalf of the recipient of the bond.

Then, if the recipient would reciprocate by accessing Heaven, requesting a saint to join the saints faith with theirs for the reception of the bonds being requested on your behalf. How powerful would that be?

The results would be exponential. The Kingdom impact would be remarkable to experience! Again, you are utilizing a cycle of faith; in this case, you are tapping into the resources of saints in Heaven, joining with saints upon the earth.

Extend this to another level. Do you suppose the saints present in the upper room would join their faith with yours for an explosive demonstration of the power of God in your church?

Do you suppose the saints from the Church of Ephesus would join their faith with yours for a Bond of Peace for your church, or the saints from Colosse, to join their faith with yours for a Bond of Maturity?

I believe we will find the answer to be yes.

Let's get started!

_____ . _____

Chapter 4

Dealing with the Bond of Iniquity

A few days later my seer and I returned to the classroom. This time our original teacher had an assistant—a much younger man named Mark.[7] We greeted them and pointed out that we wanted to continue our class time about bonds. Immediately, he began to teach us on a very different class of bonds.

What is the Bond of Iniquity

Heaven informed us that a Bond of Iniquity[8] was a lesser bond than the others. It increases the likelihood of one's life being diverted. It often attaches through the mouth (via words spoken) or through sorcery or witchcraft. It brings hardship to many people—their descendants and their lives. It is used to harm a life and

---

[7] Mark is a man in white linen who tutored us.
[8] "For I perceive that thou art in the gall of bitterness, and in the Bond of Iniquity." Acts 8:23 (KJV)

can be established in a ritual. Usually, in the ritual, death (in some fashion) is involved.

Our tutor explained that we were correct in thinking that it forms a bond, which is like *a band that keeps one from their given ability*. It keeps them back from what they are called to do. The enemy uses it quite often—more than we think.

For many, the Bond of Iniquity is a precipice. The term precipice[9] describes a situation on the brink of a significant change or potential disaster. It refers to a critical point where a decision or action could lead to a dramatic or potentially irreversible outcome. The usage conveys a sense of urgency and the need for careful consideration before taking action. This is what a Bond of Iniquity is. It is a precipice.

"How so?" You may wonder. What if you were on the edge of a cliff and suddenly someone pushed you off? Would that have been iniquitous behavior? Yes, it would. Many people stand on the edge of disaster and have a decision to make.

Why do so many plunge down the steep cliff of disaster purposely? Is it because they do not know the danger? No! They know, and they are predisposed to do so. Many have iniquitous patterns in their bloodline that predispose them to certain behaviors. The earmark of iniquity is that one has performed a particular sinful

---

[9] Precipice description" Precipice. ChatGPT August 3 Version, OpenAI, August 23, 2023, chat.opentai.com/chat

behavior for so long that it is no longer a sin to them. They are no longer convicted of their behavior.

Another reason people plunge down the steep cliff of iniquity is their arrogance. Arrogance[10] is when someone thinks they are better, smarter, or more important than others. It is like they believe they know everything and do not need to listen to anyone else. Arrogant people often act like they are too good to learn from others or consider different points of view. Being confident is good, but arrogance goes beyond that and can make it hard for people to get along with or work with that person. It is important to be humble and treat everyone with respect, no matter how much you know or how good you are at something. Many are tied to iniquitous behavior, but many leap off the cliff.

If you were standing at the bottom of a waterfall and you jumped in the water, would it be as dangerous as if you had jumped from the top? It likely would not. However, it would still be dangerous. If you were to jump regularly into the pool of water at the bottom of the waterfall and no harm came to you, you would start to think that there is no harm in that behavior. You become confident, and from that confidence, many become arrogant, thinking they cannot experience harm by their actions, but even the smallest iniquities are dangerous.

---

[10] "Arrogance description" Arrogance. ChatGPT August 3 Version, OpenAI, August 23, 2023, chat.opentai.com/chat

Tethers

Many times, iniquity tethers us. Some are predisposed to more bonds of iniquity than others based on the generational line, but all is not lost. If we were to jump in the pool at the bottom of the waterfall, would we prefer to jump from a dark or lighted place? Of course, we would prefer the lighted place. Is there a choice in arrogance? Yes, there is.

If a Bond of Iniquity comes from the generational line and arrogance makes the person not believe their actions could hurt them, the person doesn't know. Their arrogance makes them ignorant.

How do we overcome arrogance and get to a point of repentance and forgiveness? By realizing destruction always follows it and asking Holy Spirit to show us if we have it. Arrogance often comes down the family line. It is important to note that confidence and self-assuredness are positive traits, and they are distinct from arrogance. Confidence is grounded in a realistic assessment of one's abilities and accomplishments. While arrogance involves an inflated sense of self-worth often not supported by evidence. We must cultivate humility, empathy, and a willingness to learn from others.

In this is a lack of humility and a tendency to believe that people are superior to others; they often do not believe there is a consequence at the end of their behavior. Iniquitous behavior cultivates over time. It cultivates more arrogance and less humility. When you forgive, be sure to forgive your generations for their arrogance. Sin is arrogant. It is an arrogance.

If someone had a Bond of Iniquity on them and they passed away, what happens to that Bond of Iniquity? Although a person has died, the Bond of Iniquity is tethered to their generations. For example, if one of your parents dies, the tether that the Bond of Iniquity contains, is connected to the next generation and the next. All are impacted somehow, and hell goes into overtime trying to reinsert the Bond of Iniquity into that generational line to divert that family line from their destiny. As we request the Writ of Severance from the Bond of Iniquity for our generations, we are undoing the done. As you request the Writ of Severance, request the severing of every tether that exists in your generational line.

However, we must realize that tethers can be attached to any of our realms—spirit, soul, or body. Genetically, we know we can have disease and so forth come down the generational line because of iniquity. We can also have behaviors that come down the generational line because of iniquity. We have genetics, and we have egos.

Acts 8:23 speaks of the man who had to Bond of Iniquity and the gall of bitterness.

The Remedy Translation reads like this:

I can see your heart is consumed with fear, insecurity and self-centeredness, filling you with jealousy, envy and resentment of anyone or anything that takes attention away from you. (Acts 8:23)

Could this be a root of narcissism? Are the Bond of Iniquity and the gall of bitterness usually tied together or does the gall of bitterness open the door for a Bond of Iniquity?

Concerning the gall of bitterness, what would be the root? Is the gall of bitterness the door opener for the Bond of Iniquity to be placed on someone's life?

The phrase "the gall of bitterness"[11] comes from the Bible, specifically from the book of Acts in the New Testament. In Acts 8:23, it's used to describe a state of wickedness or a negative attitude. The word "gall" refers to something very bitter or poisonous, and when combined with "bitterness," it emphasizes a profoundly negative and harmful state of mind or behavior.

Metaphorically, "the gall of bitterness" refers to harboring and holding onto strong negative emotions like anger, resentment, and hostility. It suggests a poisonous and unforgiving attitude that can affect both the person holding onto these emotions and those around them. The phrase is often used to caution against allowing negative feelings to fester and harm one's well-being and relationships.

---

[11] "The Gall of Bitterness description" Gall of Bitterness. ChatGPT August 3 Version, OpenAI, August 23, 2023, chat.opentai.com/chat

Where does bitterness lie? That is the key. Does it lie in the heart (spirit) or the soul?

In Ephesians 4:31, it says:

Get rid of all bitterness, rage and anger, brawling and slander along with every form of malice. Be kind and compassionate to one another, forgiving each other. Just as Christ forgave you.

Hebrews 12:15 says,

See to it that no one falls short of the grace of God and that no bitter root grows up to cause trouble and defile many.

James 3:14-15 says:

But if you harbor bitter envy and selfish ambition in your hearts, do not boast about it. Such wisdom does not come down from heaven, but is earthly, unspiritual, and demonic.

Remember who the father of lies is—Satan. Who is the most bitter? Satan, of course.

We must remove the bitter root. However, the bitter root can be passed down or begin in a family line by unforgiveness and strong, negative emotions, resentment, or hostility. It poisons us, and it tethers us.

How do we remove the bitter root? You must plunge in deep and get to the absolute root. That is why working and aligning our realms is so important. We can deal with the root-level issues by working with each of our realms. We can remove the root. We can bring healing to our body and soul, and we can bring wholeness to all our realms.

We are to repent for the arrogance first and foremost, for the bitterness for and allowing it to rule and govern and for being tethered to arrogance and these other things. We must face these demons to remove them. We must *not* keep these things in our hearts. If it is generational, then remember that bitterness begets bitterness, arrogance begets arrogance, and so on. By doing generational work, we are stopping the madness. We are stopping the continuing momentum of this as we face the demons.

> *Your Honor, I bring all my generations in here, and I repent for the arrogance of believing we could stand on the precipice of our lives and take dangerous plunges of iniquity and not be above being reprimanded or not repenting on behalf of the deep bitterness against God in the generations.*
>
> *These deep, bitter roots stem from the father of lies. We repent for partnering with a father of lies.*
>
> *We recognize this comes from the Tree of the Knowledge of Good and Evil. Bitterness is rooted in the Tree of the Knowledge of Good and Evil.*
>
> *We repent for being bitter against God and then believing lies and having them take root and be passed down from generation to generation.*

We will repent for the arrogance and the tethering family to family and generation to generation. We kept these things in our hearts and our souls. I am asking to face these demons, and I say as a governing son, as I have offered up this repentance on behalf of my generations and myself, whereby we have allowed or partnered with the father of lies in agreeing with the root of bitterness, and it has created the Bond of Iniquity in my family line, I repent. I ask for the blood of Jesus to cover these sins. I forgive, bless, and release my generations. I face you demons, and I say, you are bound in the name of Jesus, and you no longer can work.

I would like for an angel to come and dig up this root of bitterness in my generations and to cut with the axe, laid to the root, the axe of forgiveness.

May it untether me and my generations from this tree in Jesus' name. I ask for this to be done in time and out of time in every age, realm, and dimension, all the way back to the hand of the Father. I ask this for every person on both sides of my generations for the gall of bitterness that we drank. I bind that from our generational line as well. We no longer drink from the gall of bitterness. I ask this to be as if it never were and to go back through me, my children, and my family's generation for that poison to be extracted from us in Jesus' name, every bit of spiritual debris, essence, and residue left behind in all these places. Let living water flow instead and let the junk be replaced with humility, love, forgiveness, confidence and self-assuredness with Christ Jesus. And to also have empathy and a willingness to learn, to replace all those other things in Jesus' name.

And Father, where we have used them, the Bond of Iniquity, the arrogance, and the root of bitterness to cause dishonor and harm to others. I forgive, bless, and release my generations. I forgive, bless, and release them in Jesus' name. And I ask for your righteous verdict and the spirit of understanding, wisdom, and knowledge in this, in Jesus' name.

Bonds for the Unsaved

"Can you give us pointers on using it on the unsaved?" we checked. They gave an example of a child who has yet to know the conviction of Holy Spirit. A parent might request a bond for the power & might of God (or power OR might) for the conviction of Holy Spirit to move in that person's life. This is tied to the resources of Heaven and the might of Heaven; better even than intercession, it releases a power and might of the Lord. It would manifest as conviction in that person's life of who they are and who Jesus is.

We desired an example of someone of college age. Our teacher expanded the illustration to requesting a bond for an entire college campus. The bond could be in the form of a recognition of the saving grace but would come through the power and might of God.

We asked if we could request a bond for an unsaved person's desire.

Bond for a Person's Desire

We sensed that these bonds were essentially unlimited, but you needed to pause and ask Holy Spirit what bond to request in each situation. Regarding the request concerning one's desire, you would request a Writ of Release for the Wooing of God. They would then be wooed to desire God. For a lost person, the best bond would depend upon their age. It also depends on the position of the person asking. If one has specific connectedness to a college campus (as in a parent or grandparent of a student or your proximity to the school, (i.e., your sphere of influence including your location, your interest, or understanding), that connectedness qualifies them to be able to ask for a bond for that college campus. It varies based on that.

We were reminded with a chuckle that we do have Holy Spirit and can ask Him for help. We need to pause and ask for what bond to use!

Bonds for those in Addiction

"What kind of bond would you recommend for someone in addiction?" we investigated. You would request for the bond of recognition of their addiction. They would then be able to recognize they have been bound by addiction; they are trapped. It would be a Bond of Clarity Concerning their Own Addiction.

For most sins, it would involve the request for a Bond of Clarity. As a result, the person would be able to see the truth, thus initiating the defeat of the lie of the enemy. We were told that the Bond of Clarity was good for people caught up in any addiction. Whatever they are turning to instead of Jesus and being caught up in that thing by way of addiction, a Bond of Clarity is a great resource to help that person.

Regardless of the addiction, the Bond of Clarity is powerful.

More Bonds for Unbelievers

"What else do we need to know about bonds for unbelievers?" That was our next question.

Our teacher responded, "Bonds may manifest differently regarding the unsaved based on the nation they are a part of and that nation's timing to honor the Lord Jesus."

Bonds are often subject to timing—the type of timing that only the Father knows, but in general, requesting a bond will always start something. It will always initiate an action in a life, but it will be after larger-framed times and seasons.

Mark told us not to fret if we have requested a bond for an unsaved person and we have yet to see the manifestation. It is not that the bond is not working, it may be under a higher framework of time of the nation the person is in. Nevertheless, it will be logged in Heaven, so when the timing happens, it's already in line to be among the first released. When Paul wanted to go to Asia but was redirected to Macedonia—that was a timing issue; this is similar. A bond is under the same framework when it comes to nations.

What is the Best Bond for the Lost?

A Bond of the Power of God with a Writ of Release of the Convicting Power of God tied to the might of Heaven. Such a bond releases the power of Heaven.

Pitfalls

"Can you show us some of the pitfalls?" we explored.

Although he had already spoken of this in our prior class, Mark reiterated that if the request for a bond for someone is not done from love or if it is done to control, then it would become an ungodly bond, and demons would respond to that bond instead of the angels of God. The demons would be happy to help you create a bond out of the court of hell *if love is not your motivation or the motivation is control.* Such a bond would be logged in Heaven *and* the court of hell.

Undoing an Ungodly Bond

Next, we wanted to explore, "How do we go about undoing an ungodly bond, as an ungodly bond in the Bond Registry book of the person or people affected?" We were instructed to:

- See it in the registry.
- Follow the protocol of forgive, bless, and release.
- Request a Writ of Severance of the ungodly bond from the Court of Titles and Deeds.
- Receive the verdict from the court.
- Access the Court of Cancellations, submitting the verdict from the prior court.
- Request the cancellation of every impact and ramification of the ungodly bonds.

Undoing a Bond of a Demon to Someone

"What about for those in darkness when a demon has been bound to someone?" we began to speculate.

- Access the Court of Cancellations and request a cancellation of the bond and all associated

writs all the way from when it was first established.
- Follow the protocol of forgiving, blessing, and releasing the one who set up the ungodly bond if they were human.[12]
- Ask the Blood of the Lamb to cover it.

Low-level witches seek to establish bonds against the president, governors, LEO's (Law Enforcement Officers), and others on every level of government through sacrifices of all sorts. Ungodly bonds are the tools they use in many situations. They are using ungodly bonds to create demonic assignments. Just as Godly bonds activate angels, ungodly bonds activate demons. Just as angels are released through godly bonds, demons are released through ungodly bonds.

A Testimony

While conducting a court session with someone, we took a short diversion to see what (if any) bonds were on the registry for me and the ministry. She saw a Bond of Chaos issued by a court of hell two months prior. As soon as that session ended, we stepped into the Court of Titles & Deeds requesting a Writ of Severance from the Bond of Chaos originating from the Court of hell.

---

[12] It is not necessary to forgive, bless, and release when these bonds were issued from a court of hell or the counsels of hell. Forgiving, blessing, and releasing applies only when dealing with humans.

Immediately, the scene changed to one of a courtroom session with attendants hustling about gathering evidence (or the lack thereof) concerning this Bond of Chaos.

The court determined that insufficient evidence existed for the bond to be in place and found "no justifiable evidence" concerning it. It was then struck down, and the Writ of Severance was issued. Once we received it, we also requested restitution to everything lost during the time frame involved—including restoration of relationships, finances, camaraderie, etc.

———·———

Chapter 5
Spiritual Booby Traps

At this point, someone else came into the classroom whose presence we could not ignore. He was a demolition expert[13] and wanted to show us something vital for this time.

He invited us to go with him to the ammunition supply depot.

He led us outdoors next to a bunker. We sensed a lot of angelic activity. Many bunkers covered the field. The angels had been storing up ammunition for a very long time. From a historical perspective, we could see dynamite, pyrotechnics of different sorts, munitions, missiles, bombs, etc., from all time periods here in storage.

We asked why we were brought to this place and were told, "To show you the capability of what can be

---

[13] We assumed this was an angel.

loosed against the witches you saw earlier." He asked us why the witches could get away with the stunts they were pulling.

The answer is, "Because we have not loosed the armaments." Some have, but he was requesting that we make it known that there is more firepower that the saints need to use—and do it on the offensive, not merely defensive. "How will these witches ever know the firepower of God unless the saints utilize the access you have been given to the armaments of Heaven?" he asked.

The seer noticed that an angel had a large pocket watch in his hand. When asked why he had the pocket watch, he replied, "It is time for the release of this from Heaven."

This angel was on assignment because it is time to release the weapons of warfare that have not been loosed—the common loosing of the weapons of warfare of the saints.

> *It is time to release the weapons of warfare that have not been loosed.*

The Scroll

We then saw a large scroll with many signatures on it. The demolition expert wanted us to sign our names on the scroll. It looked like the Declaration of Independence. It was like a petition—it needed a number of saints who would agree to sign off on it so it could become a legal decree. The Father had already signed off on it but wanted more signatories on it so that more saints could become aware of their access to release the armaments of Heaven. We were told the earth is suffering violence because the saints are not releasing the armaments of Heaven.

These armaments are supernatural and affect many realms—seen and unseen. They affect the trade routes between the realms that many witches use (even immature ones).

We asked if we needed to sign the document and asked for the name of the document. We were told it was an "Agreement for the Release of the Armaments of Heaven." We signed it.

The Spiritual Booby Trap

We noticed he now had a booby trap, and he explained how this would become common—yet currently, it is a little-used weapon. It is not hard to use it to release a booby trap against the enemies of Yahweh in the spiritual realms.

It will contain the witches and make them think twice about releasing ungodly bonds. He wanted us to learn how to do this.

Releasing Spiritual Booby Traps

We asked, "Do we do this from the aspect of the Courts?"

It was explained to us that we can do it *vocally in prayer*. We were told that we could set them around individuals and set them around cities simply by prayer and a vocal decree. We can set them against illegal trespassers in the spirit realm by vocal decree. We can set them over cities, especially if we have authority for that city (meaning we are a part of it).

What Happens?

When the ungodly loose an ungodly bond against an individual, a city, or a group like a college campus, if we have already been to that place to lay the booby trap, then when they place the bond, by their action, they get trapped—they walk *into* a trap.

Using the Courts to Set Traps

Believers can access the Court of Decrees, where you can see the map of places available to put these booby traps. The Court of Decrees has a Strategy Room to which you can sign in. We can enter the Strategy Room and request to know if we have been granted authority to release booby traps over regions, and if you have, they will show you the map where you have been given clearance to set traps.

The Court of Decrees will have information in the Strategy Room on where booby traps are needed.

Coming into agreement with the decree is a form of signing off on the decree.

Clearance for the Strategy Room

Heaven knows if you have the authority to access the Strategy Room. Clearance to this Strategy Room comes because of practice—because you have sought it and because of your responsible stewardship. You are allowed to come in and look to see if you have clearance for the task at hand. If you come in to see if you have clearance, but you don't, it's OK. Once you have clearance, you are authorized to obtain the placement for the booby traps.

The authorization aspect is to keep the immature out of this process. You need to have walked in some maturity to gain clearance.

I can access the Strategy Room to request access and clearance to set booby traps. If I have access, I can see the map for the region with the activity where the booby traps need to be set. I can then request that the decree be issued from the court.

What is the Protocol?

1. Access the Court of Decrees complex.
2. Access the Strategy Room.
3. If you have clearance, you can see the map for the region with activity needing the booby traps.
4. Request the decree for them be issued from the Court of Decree by agreement, in the name of Jesus.
5. Once approval is granted, receive the decree, and establish it in the earth by vocalizing it.

Doing this carries greater authority and specific knowledge when you do it in the courts. It is the difference between sniping (using a high-caliber rifle) and using a shotgun.

The reason we had come to that place was because we saw the witch's activity and needed to know about this weaponry.

——— · ———

Shirley's Testimony

I overheard Dr. Ron working with a lady who had come requesting a Bond of Financial Provision for someone, so I heard Holy Spirit say to request one for my daughter, so I just said what I heard Dr. Ron say.

The next morning, I got a call from my daughter, who is attending college, saying the finance office had called to tell her she had $200 in her account. A little while later, they called to let her know an additional $200 was in her account. My daughter and I were both excited about this.

Editor's note:

Before leaving school that day, the daughter checked her account for herself and discovered it had over $1,000 in it! Praise God!

Chapter 6

Back in the Classroom

We were asked if we wanted to know what a Bond of Theft was. Of course, we answered yes. Our tutor then proceeded to give us understanding.

Bond of Theft

The enemy has a version of the Bond of Iniquity called the Bond of Theft. When a bloodline begins trading in thieving (whether material or immaterial goods such as reputation, status, etc.) or someone in the bloodline tries to steal favor, the enemy, who hunts for someone who is lusting after someone else's goods, status, reputation, etc. gets this iniquity linked to a generational line. It is like a backlash for the one who originated this bond by their lusts.

First, they get stuck in the cycle of lusting; then, a bond is created by Satan, affecting the entire generational line. When God says, "Do not covet," it is because He knows that coveting can initiate this writ in the bloodline, thus permitting the enemy to steal from it.

Our tutor outlined a couple of things we refer to as results of iniquity:

- They can't hold on to their seed.
- They can't hold onto their acquisitions.
- They lose favor with God and man.

These are the results of the Bond of Theft.

The Bond of Theft is registered in hell *and* Heaven's registry. We can look for it in the Office of Registry within the Court of Records.

Steps to Freedom from a Bond of Theft

- Request access to the Court of Titles and Deeds.
- Request a Writ of Severance of the Bond of Theft.
- Follow the protocol of forgiveness:
    - Forgive
    - Bless
    - Release
- Repent for the coveting in the generations—those who initiated and perpetuated it.
- Request the Blood of Jesus be applied to the situation and a Writ of Severance be issued to all attached to that bond by blood, marriage, adoption, civil, or religious covenant from all the impacts and the ramifications of that Bond of Theft.

- Receive the Writ of Severance (spend a moment grasping the magnitude of the Writ of Severance regarding the ungodly bond).
- Receive the verdict from the court.
- Access the Court of Cancellations, submitting the verdict from the prior court.
- Request the cancellation of every impact and ramification of the ungodly bonds.
- Receive the verdict.

We asked, "What would a Bond of Theft look like in the Old Testament?"

The answer was, "David's lusting after Bathsheba resulted in this bond being created and resulted in the death of the child."

That was all our class for that day. We thanked our tutors and received permission to return another day.

———·———

A Testimony

I had my second bonds registry session with Karee, Elizabeth, and CeCe yesterday. The afternoon before the session, I started to come down with cold and flu-like symptoms, but I did not want to come into agreement with these. I loved, blessed, forgave, and released an unwell and sneezing sister in Christ whom I had been in a meeting with a few nights earlier. The battle not to accept the symptoms persisted throughout my workday afternoon, and during it, as I prayed in the spirit and released blessings and scriptures, I asked out loud for the angelic hosts with capture bags and color frequencies to be released as I understood it was a spiritual attack coming against my session for the next day. Something opened in the spirit. I saw it first as a golden, light angel holding a pink pouch for being rosy cheeked and in the pink of health. I suddenly flashed into a room in Heaven which I understood was Heaven's Sanitorium. Here, I received refreshment, re-tuning, and alignment from colored 'Refreshment Pouches' from personnel under the auspices of "Dr. Jesus." I think this was because a few months ago I had declared that my doctor was Dr. Jesus, and my hospital was in Heaven!

There was also a blue pouch that contained rest and rejuvenation by the ocean in it and I relaxed there for a short time, bearing in mind that I was still at work on Earth. There was a green pouch that had growth and herbs in it. From the green pouch, I understood it had healing from the Tree of Life in it and then I saw that when the dove flew back to the ark after the flood, the branch in its beak had roots on it and it was actually from the Tree of Life to re-seed the Earth from Heaven in the spirit. I have an affinity with the dove emblem because the church the Lord sent me to is at St Columba (Colmcille—dove). In a few Earth seconds, I was back in the Earth realm, refreshed and with the symptoms of cold and flu-like reactions much decreased.

As I stepped outside of my workplace in an industrial area, there was a strong chemical substance and a smell in the air like extra-potent glue from a factory. I have had major chemical sensitivity issues in the past with many years of sickness from inhaled spray from our family farm and the next-door orchard as a child. I prayed for protection on the way home from allergens, pathogens, etc., and for my chemical receptor function to be restored. The Lord reminded me that when I had been in Heaven's Sanitorium, I had received a light clothing of gold, and this was for protection from these types of substances. As I was driving home, I was drawn to look at the number plate of another oncoming vehicle—it read Zoe. I started laughing and declaring out loud—Zoe Life!!! The Lord reminded me I had been declaring the Scripture that He is the Way, the Truth, and the Life. By the time I got home, I had almost no symptoms, but I could perceive them wafting around me outside a protective barrier. The symptoms could not touch me if I did not agree with them.

This is important in my life because I had spent many years in hospital as a teenager with a rare immune disease, known as Henoch Schonlein Nephritis Purpura, in which my bodily system *attacked its own organs in a misplaced response to colds, flu, and chemical sensitivities. I had suffered much from the ages of 12 until my mid-50s with this, including a time during which both kidneys had failed, and multiple organs had been severely compromised—very debilitating. The Lord has been healing me miraculously and progressively over the past 4-5 years and this experience of the Heavenly Sanitorium and Refreshment Pouches through LifeSpring Ministries is at another level entirely, following on from having ungodly bonds removed and Godly bonds released.*

Glory to God and thank you for the work you are co-laboring in with the Heavenly Realms, by the grace of our Lord Jesus Christ.

Your sister in Christ,
LK
Auckland, New Zealand

Chapter 7

Understanding the Registry

Heaven makes it relatively simple to determine when things are affecting our lives. Knowing what bonds are in effect over our lives is one of those areas we can easily discover. This is one of the many registries you want to know about in this office.

Office of Registry

Within the Court of Records is the Office of Registry. Within this office, you can request to see your Registry of Bonds. It will include any bond that has been placed over your life—Godly or ungodly. The book generally appears as a leather-bound ancient book with gold leaf or embossing on the cover entitled *Registry*. As you open it (and it seems to open from the top rather than the side), you will see the paper divided into two columns. On the left are the Godly bonds that have been requested for your life by others. In the right column are the ungodly bonds affecting your life.

Pages in the Bond Registry

We had learned in a Personal Advocacy Session in the courts the day before that each registry has several pages:

- A Personal page.
- A Family page.
- A Business/Ministry/Education page.
- A Relationship page (relatives, groups, friendships, etc.).

We had some questions about these various pages.

Personal Page

Often when you see an ungodly bond in the right column of the registry, it will be an attempt by darkness to counteract or neutralize a Godly bond in the left column of your registry. For example, if you find in the left column a Bond of Freedom, you will often find a Bond of Slavery (or something similar) listed in the right column. The idea is to slow down your ability to receive the beneficial bond in the left column by *trying to place a hindrance in your life*.

The steps to freedom are simple, and we have listed them in a previous chapter. At times you may see a bond listed, but the listing is not in color or is greyed out. That seems to indicate that it is not currently active for some reason. In any event, you will want to dispose of it by following the Steps to Freedom (see the previous chapter), so it cannot impact your life.

Family Page

If you find a bond on your registry's Family page, you will likely find the same bond on your spouse or children's individual pages. Once you clear it from your registry, the Lord, in His great mercy, *clears it from all the immediate family where it had been placed.* Hallelujah!

---
*Once you clear a bond
from your registry,
the Lord in His great mercy,
clears it from all the immediate family
where it had been placed.*

In a ministry session, we were encouraged that when we effected the removal of an ungodly bond, we needed to request its counterpart immediately if none previously existed. Again, using the example of a Bond of Bondage, the counterpart would be a Bond of Freedom; if a Bond of Fear, then a Bond of Love as a countermeasure. Simply listen to the instruction of Holy Spirit. He always knows what is best. Don't fall into the trap of using your mind to simply look for an item's antonym. Follow Holy Spirits' instruction.

When removing an ungodly bond from a family, it is always removed from the immediate family (i.e., spouse, children, and parents.) Should the individual not be married, it is removed from them, their offspring, and their parents, however, not necessarily from siblings. This has to do with the siblings' choice of walk, but the grace of God affects only the immediate line for this page.

With an unmarried person, it would be removed from them and their parents but not their siblings. However, it would be logged in Heaven that there is freedom in that line. An ease for the dissolution of the bond for the siblings would come, as well as ease in other ways.

Business/Ministry Page

An ungodly bond against a business must always be viewed considering what the business is trading. The individual trades could have bonds against them, or the entire business could have an ungodly bond. A ministry could have an ungodly bond, or its trades could have ungodly bonds against them. This would be due to evil activity choosing the level of opposition, whether they are coming against the trade of the business, ministry, or entity or perhaps against the business, ministry, or entity itself.

It requires a lot more work on the part of evil to loose these ungodly bonds against a business, ministry, or entity. It takes more work for them to keep the ungodly bond in place against the entire business than it does against the individual trade. *It is easier for them to come against a trade than to come against an entire business.* The degree of work it requires means they are *more likely to focus on an individual trade than the entire business.* It takes more work for them to accomplish it and maintain it in the spirit realm, but you can often see ungodly bonds established by evil against a specific trade.

Ministries:

What are common ungodly bonds ministries deal with?

Bond of Division – to interfere with their progress.

Bond of Cloaking – to make the ministry invisible.

Bond of Derision – this makes the rest of humanity mock them, consider them irrelevant, or casts dispersion on them.

The bonds can be targeted to the ministry itself or their trades. For example, if a ministry decides to have a particular outreach or thrust, then the witches could come against that trade with ungodly bonds and not have to come against the entire ministry.

Mark, our tutor's assistant, began to teach us at this point.

Relationships Page

What are common ungodly bonds against relationships?

Bond of Division – Keeps them from moving forward in unity.

Bond of Prickliness – The persons cannot see eye to eye, cannot get close. This often happens suddenly.

Bond of Scarcity – Keeps people apart in time and connection, time they spend together, or time spent thinking of the other.

Bond of Lack – (Lack is different from scarcity which refers to the time they spend together or time they spend thinking of the other.) Lack hinders them from sharing resources, ideas, dreams, etc. with each other- the things you would build a relationship with. It serves as a black hole where suddenly you stop sharing those things, and the relationship suffers.

Bond of Displeasure – This predisposes the people in the relationship to find fault and judge each other.

The opposite of these ungodly bonds is what you want to ask a Godly bond for. For instance:

Bond of Lack <> Bond of Plenty or Bond of Deep Sharing

Bond of Displeasure <> Bond of Esteem or Bond of Honor or Bond of Respect

More Godly bonds exist than are available to darkness as the counterpart (or that they are currently using).

Bonds are wonderful things! It's the Father's pleasure.

> *There is so much pleasure in Heaven when the saints ask for bonds.*

The Bond Department hasn't been busy for a while. It has been empty. The Bond Department is the back end where these things are recorded, worked out, angels released, assignments given, or noted from where evil bonds were established.

What About Businesses

Sometime later, we began applying the same concepts to businesses/ministries. The pages were similar but adapted to the setting.

For instance:

- Personal Page became the page for the principal personnel/managers or the Employers Page in the business or ministry.
- Family Page became the Employee's Page.
- Business/Ministry/Education page dealt with the entity itself.
- Relationships Page became Vendors/Clients/Customers, etc.

Business Pages:

- Principals/Personnel/Management Team
- Employees/Contractors/Team
- The entity itself.
- Vendors/Clients/Customers

Then, we utilized the same principles for dealing with them and requesting Godly bonds for the business/ministry.

Chapter 8
Sample Writs

Writs are the paperwork defining a bond. It is a specific request—essentially a one-liner that summarizes what you want for the other party. On the following pages are examples of writs that you can use. Writs are simply orders issued by the courts on behalf of the plaintiff (you).

Following each writ is the recommendation to perform a prophetic act of receiving the writ from the Judge and placing that writ into your heart. If you visualize this as it is happening, it will solidify that Heaven has acted on behalf of the request you have just made in the Court of Titles and Deeds. Remember to be respectful of the Judge and the personnel in the courtroom. What you honor, you will have the benefit of. Always keep that in mind as you engage in the Courts of Heaven.

Also, we have included a place for you to list who you have obtained writs for and the date you did so. Over time this should be quite a faith builder for you.

Writ of Release of the Extravagant Love of God (Bond of Love)

I request access to the Court of Titles & Deeds on this day.

I am requesting a Writ of Release of the Extravagant Love of God toward _____.

I request this Bond on his/her/their behalf today, in Jesus' name.

I now receive this Bond into my heart on their behalf, in Jesus' name. Thank You.

[I recommend you perform a prophetic act of receiving the Writ from the Judge and receive it into your heart. Visualizing these things will help solidify them in your life.]

Utilized on behalf of: *Date:*

_____

_____

_____

_____

Writ of Release of Marital Unity
(Bond of Body)

I request access to the Court of Titles & Deeds this day.

I am requesting a Writ of Release of Marital Unity for _____.

I request this Bond on his/her/their behalf today, in Jesus' name.

I now receive this Bond into my heart in their behalf, in Jesus' name. Thank You.

[I recommend you perform a prophetic act of receiving the Writ from the Judge and receive it into your heart. As you visualize these things it will help solidify them in your life.]

Utilized on behalf of: *Date:*

_____

_____

_____

_____

Writ of Release of Maternal Love
(Bond of Maternal Love)

I request access to the Court of Titles & Deeds this day.

I am requesting a Writ of Release of Maternal Love between _____ and her child/children _____.

I request this Bond on his/her/their behalf today, in Jesus' name.

I now receive this Bond into my heart on their behalf, in Jesus' name. Thank You.

[I recommend you perform a prophetic act of receiving the Writ from the Judge and receive it into your heart. Visualizing these things will help solidify them in your life.]

Utilized on behalf of: Date:

_____

_____

_____

_____

_____

Writ of Release of Healing
(Bond of Healing)

I request access to the Court of Titles & Deeds on this day.

I am requesting a Writ of Release of Healing of Every Infirmity Affecting _____'s body, soul, and spirit.

I request this Bond on his/her/their behalf today, in Jesus' name.

I now receive this Bond into my heart on their behalf, in Jesus' name. Thank You.

[I recommend you perform a prophetic act of receiving the Writ from the Judge and receive it into your heart. Visualizing these things will help solidify them in your life.]

Utilized on behalf of: Date:

_____

_____

_____

_____

Writ of Release of Clarity
(Bond of Clarity)

I request access to the Court of Titles & Deeds on this day.

I am requesting a Bond of Clarity—specifically a Writ of Release of Clarity Toward Your Purposes for _____.

I request this Bond on his/her/their behalf today, in Jesus' name.

I now receive this Bond into my heart on their behalf, in Jesus' name. Thank You.

[I recommend you perform a prophetic act of receiving the Writ from the Judge and receive it into your heart. Visualizing these things will help solidify them in your life.]

Utilized on behalf of: *Date:*

_____

_____

_____

_____

Writ of Release of Wisdom
(Bond of Wisdom)

I request access to the Court of Titles & Deeds on this day.

I also request a Writ of Release of Wisdom for _____.

I request this Bond on his/her/their behalf today, in Jesus' name.

I now receive this Bond into my heart on their behalf, in Jesus' name. Thank You.

[I recommend you perform a prophetic act of receiving the Writ from the Judge and receive it into your heart. Visualizing these things will help solidify them in your life.]

Utilized on behalf of: Date:

_____

_____

_____

_____

Writ of Release of Creativity
(Bond of Creativity)

I request access to the Court of Titles & Deeds on this day.

I also request a "Writ of Release of Creativity for _____.

I request this Bond on his/her/their behalf today, in Jesus' name.

I now receive this Bond into my heart on their behalf, in Jesus' name. Thank You.

[I recommend you perform a prophetic act of receiving the Writ from the Judge and receive it into your heart. Visualizing these things will help solidify them in your life.]

Utilized on behalf of: *Date:*

_____

_____

_____

_____

Writ of Release of Peace
(Bond of Peace)

I request access to the Court of Titles & Deeds on this day.

I am requesting a Writ of Release of Peace for _____.

I request this Bond on his/her/their behalf today, in Jesus' name.

I now receive this Bond into my heart on their behalf, in Jesus' name. Thank You.

[I recommend you perform a prophetic act of receiving the Writ from the Judge and receive it into your heart. Visualizing these things will help solidify them in your life.]

Utilized on behalf of: *Date:*

_____

_____

_____

_____

Writ of Release of Maturity
(Bond of Maturity/Perfection)

I request access to the Court of Titles & Deeds on this day.

I am requesting a Writ of Release of Maturity on Behalf of _____.

I request this Bond on his/her/their behalf today, in Jesus' name.

I now receive this Bond into my heart on their behalf, in Jesus' name. Thank You.

[I recommend you perform a prophetic act of receiving the Writ from the Judge and receive it into your heart. Visualizing these things will help solidify them in your life.]

Utilized on behalf of: Date:

_____

_____

_____

_____

_____

Writ of Release of Finances
(Bond of Healing)

I request access to the Court of Titles & Deeds on this day.

I am requesting a Writ of Release of Finances for _____.

I request this Bond on his/her/their behalf today, in Jesus' name.

I now receive this Bond into my heart on their behalf, in Jesus' name. Thank You.

[I recommend you perform a prophetic act of receiving the Writ from the Judge and receive it into your heart. Visualizing these things will help solidify them in your life.]

Utilized on behalf of: Date:

_____

_____

_____

_____

_____

Writ of Release of Safety
(Bond of Safety)

I request access to the Court of Titles & Deeds on this day.

I am requesting a Writ of Release of Safety for _____.

I request this Bond on his/her/their behalf today, in Jesus' name.

I now receive this Bond into my heart on their behalf, in Jesus' name. Thank You.

[I recommend you perform a prophetic act of receiving the Writ from the Judge and receive it into your heart. Visualizing these things will help solidify them in your life.]

Utilized on behalf of: *Date:*

_____

_____

_____

_____ . _____

Chapter 9
Writ of Severance

Obtaining relief from ungodly bonds is imperative for us to move into the arenas God has for our lives. We will provide a few scenarios on the following pages to help you walk through the process. Always be sensitive to Holy Spirit in case He wants to interject something or have you repent of something for yourself or someone else.

Writ of Severance

Concerning a Writ of Bondage

[It is sometimes helpful to have someone assist you in case you need a bond issued on your behalf to counteract any ungodly bond that is discovered]

I request access to the Court of Titles and Deeds. I am requesting a Writ of Severance from the Writ of Bondage that has been placed upon my life. I forgive the one who placed it on my life. I bless them, and I release them, in Jesus' name.

I repent for every sin that may have allowed this in my life or generations. I ask your forgiveness, in Jesus' name.

[Watch what happens in this situation in the Court. When the Writ of Severance is issued, receive it into your heart. Pause momentarily to meditate on the magnitude of this Writ of Severance you just received. Then proceed to the Court of Cancellations.]

If no counteracting bond was found in your registry, request the person helping you to request a Bond of (<u>whatever is a counteracting bond</u>) on your behalf.

I request access to the Court of Cancellations. I am requesting the cancellation of the ungodly Bond of Bondage and the cancellation of every impact and ramification that this Bond of Bondage has had on my life. I request restitution of everything lost and that every Godly bond over my life be released to fulfill its intent. In Jesus' name, I ask.

[Now receive what has been done on your behalf. Remember to be sensitive to

Holy Spirit to follow any instructions given.]

Writ of Severance Concerning a Writ of Poverty

[It is sometimes helpful to have someone assist you in case you need a bond issued on your behalf to counteract any ungodly bond that is discovered]

I request access to the Court of Titles and Deeds. I request a Writ of Severance from the Writ of Poverty placed upon my life. I forgive the one who placed it there. I bless them, and I release them, in Jesus' name.

I repent for every sin that may have allowed this in my life or generations. I ask your forgiveness, in Jesus' name.

[Watch what happens in this situation in the Court. When the Writ of Severance is issued, receive it into your heart. Pause momentarily to meditate on the magnitude of this Writ of Severance you just received. Then proceed to the Court of Cancellations.]

I request access to the Court of Cancellations. I am requesting the cancellation of the ungodly Bond of Poverty and the cancellation of every impact and ramification that this Bond of Poverty has had on my life. I request restitution of everything lost, and that every Godly bond over my life be released to fulfill its intent. In Jesus' name, I ask.

[Now receive what has been done on your behalf. Remember to be sensitive to Holy Spirit to follow any instructions given.]

You can take this simple format and tailor it to the situation of the person you are doing this on behalf of. The following sample is fill-in-the-blank:

Writ of Severance

Concerning a Writ of _____

[It is sometimes helpful to have someone assist you in case you need a bond issued on your behalf to counteract any ungodly bond that is discovered]

I request access to the Court of Titles and Deeds. I am requesting a Writ of Severance from the Writ of_____ that has been placed upon my life. I forgive the one who placed it on my life. I bless them, and I release them, in Jesus' name.

I repent for every sin that may have allowed this in my life or generations. I ask your forgiveness, in Jesus' name.

[Watch what happens in this situation in the Court. When the Writ of Severance is issued, receive it into your heart. Pause momentarily to meditate on the magnitude of this Writ of Severance you just received. Then proceed to the Court of Cancellations.]

I request access to the Court of Cancellations. I am requesting the cancellation of the ungodly Bond of _____ and the cancellation of every impact and ramification that this Bond of_____ has had on my life. I request restitution of everything lost and that every Godly bond over my life be released to fulfill its intent. In Jesus' name, I ask.

[Now receive what has been done on your behalf. Remember to be sensitive to Holy Spirit to follow any instructions given.]

_____ . _____

Another Testimony

I had my first Bond Registry session with Karee and the team one month ago. A lot has happened in the past month, as they said it would. I divorced from a water spirit, which made things much clearer! Whenever the enemy tried to put things back on me that had been cleared from the ungodly bonds on my personal and family pages and for ministry and business, I could resist and not come into agreement with this and declare my Godly bonds whenever I started to doubt. When they asked me if I would like any Godly bonds, I asked for courage and boldness to preach the gospel and share Jesus with people. Standing on my new Godly bonds, I went out on the street and shared and prayed with strangers the next day. This broke an almost 60-year drought! I was in a little Glory bubble and not afraid. My spiritual senses were highly attuned, and I started flashing into various rooms of Heaven. I felt peace and purpose and I knew my Heavenly Father indeed loves me, and my relationship with Father, Son, and Holy Spirit deepened as I experienced the Godly bonds in action.

Blessings,
LK

Chapter 10
Various Bonds

What is hidden will be revealed! This is a promise repeated several times in the Word of God. Since revelation always brings revolution, we are excited about the revolution this revelation will bring forth. In this chapter, we outline some of the various types of ungodly bonds you might encounter to give you a frame of reference. Then we list the numerous Godly Bonds we have encountered thus far. Hopefully, this will help you recognize the potential arenas of impact of bonds on others' lives and also give you ideas of bonds you can release on behalf of others. A more exhaustive list of each type of bond is found in the Appendix.

Ungodly Bonds

Bond of Affliction	Bond of Bondage
Bond of Anger & Rage	Bond of Calcification
Bond of Betrayal	Bond of Catastrophe

- Bond of Chaos
- Bond of Cunning & Trickery
- Bond of Deception
- Bond of Derision
- Bond of Destruction
- Bond of Detriment
- Bond of Deviation
- Bond of Deviation of Grace
- Bond of Divination
- Bond of Divisiveness
- Bond of Entanglement
- Bond of Failure
- Bond of Forlorn
- Bond of Galactical Substances
- Bond of Hardship
- Bond of Hatred
- Bond of Hesitation
- Bond of Ill Health
- Bond of Inflammation
- Bond of Iniquity
- Bond of Injustice
- Bond of Mockery
- Bond of Not Having Accountability
- Bond of Obliviousness
- Bond of Ovation
- Bond of Procrastination
- Bond of Restraint
- Bond of Sarcasm
- Bond of Self-Effort
- Bond of Self-exaltation
- Bond of Self-Hatred
- Bond of Severing
- Bond of Shearing
- Bond of Sorrow
- Bond of Stagnation
- Bond of Strife
- Bond of Synchronized Chaos
- Bond of Synchronized Destruction

Bond of Theft

Bond of Thievery

Bond of Tragedy

Bond of Transference

Bond of Trepidation

Bond of Ungodly Time

Bond of Wicked Illumination

Bond of Wicked Schemes

Bond of a Yoke of Sadness

Godly Bonds

Bond of A Heart for the Lord

Bond of A Sound Mind

Bond of Accelerated Healing

Bond of Adoption

Bond of Authority in the Business Arena

Bond of Blessing

Bond of Clarity

Bond of Commerce

Bond of Creativity

Bond of Creativity in Giving

Bond of Dancing

Bond of Demonstration

Bond of Dependence Upon God

Bond of Destiny

Bond of Discernment

Bond of Divine Guidance

Bond of Doing Things from the Seat of Rest

Bond of Embrace of New Paradigm

Bond of Energy

Bond of Entrepreneurship

Bond of Excellence

- Bond of Expansion
- Bond of Exponential Increase
- Bond of Favor
- Bond of Financial Provision
- Bond of Fortitude
- Bond of Free Flow of Exchange of Ideas
- Bond of Freedom
- Bond of Friendship
- Bond of Fruitfulness
- Bond of Generosity
- Bond of Giftings, Anointings, Revelations of God
- Bond of Goodness
- Bond of Grace
- Bond of Healing
- Bond of Health
- Bond of Holiness
- Bond of Hope
- Bond of Humility
- Bond of Illumination
- Bond of Inheritance
- Bond of Joy
- Bond of Knowledge
- Bond of Leverage
- Bond of Love
- Bond of Matrimony
- Bond of Maturity
- Bond of Melting of Frozen Hearts
- Bond of Mental Wholeness
- Bond of Mercy
- Bond of Miracles
- Bond of Mutual Agreement/Unity
- Bond of Networking
- Bond of Open-mindedness
- Bond of Opportunity
- Bond of Patience
- Bond of Peace
- Bond of Persistence
- Bond of Physical Restoration
- Bond of Power & Might
- Bond of Praise
- Bond of Progress
- Bond of Promise

- Bond of Prosperity
- Bond of Protection
- Bond of Protection of Health
- Bond of Provision
- Bond of Redemption
- Bond of Restoration
- Bond of Sacraments
- Bond of Safety
- Bond of Sensitivity to Holy Spirit
- Bond of Signs & Wonders
- Bond of Sonship
- Bond of Strategy
- Bond of Supernatural Provisions
- Bond of Sweeping Change
- Bond of Swiftness
- Bond of the Blueprints of Heaven
- Bond of the Extravagant Love of God
- Bond of the Fear of the Lord
- Bond of the Frequencies of Heaven
- Bond of the Joy of the Lord
- Bond of Trade
- Bond of Tranquility
- Bond of Transition
- Bond of Transparency
- Bond of Travel
- Bond of True Discernment
- Bond of Unity
- Bond of Unity for the Family
- Bond of Wellness
- Bond of Wholeness
- Bond of Wisdom
- Bond of Yoked to the Lord

——— · ———

Chapter 11
Working with Bond Registry Angels

We asked permission to return to the Help Desk, as we rechecked it for the ministry. We wanted to know if anything was on our schedule.

The words "Bond Registry" were heard, but we were unsure what was being said. We asked for clarification.

"Could someone come and help talk to us about a Bond Registry and angels?" we asked.

Lydia[14] came and explained that she wanted to discuss the book's revelation regarding the bonds and the Bond Registry. She gave us a new understanding of the angels and the Bond Registry.

We learned that in the Court of Records, we have seen assistants who have brought out registries to us, helped

---

[14] Lydia is a woman in white who advises our ministry.

us turn pages, and given us counsel. They are angels assigned to oversee registries of individuals and entities. These angels on duty in the Office of Records are also connected to an army of angels. They take turns working in the Bond Registry Office and carrying out the release of Godly bonds requested in the courts and on bond registries of individuals and entities. By their design, the Bond Registry is very dear to them. They are grieved when ungodly bonds are assigned but elated when the saints work from courtroom realms to deal with bonds. *They are on assignment to enact the outplay of Godly bonds assigned* as courtroom work is done by saints filling bond registries with the Godly bonds.

Their activity escalates exponentially because of the filling of Bond Registry pages with Godly bonds. They have a specific type of expression or flavor. They have a particular resonance about them because of their assignment.

These angels are assigned to the Bond Registry, so they have a particular manner about them. Even their stature and velocity are designed to be related to what they do regarding the Bond Registry. They are responsible for bringing people an understanding of the Bond Registry. They are responsible for hearing and receiving the orders of the courts where bonds are released to people, and they bring that bond's expression into a person's life.

For example, a bond of peace released for a person through the courtroom work of the saints releases a

Bond Registry Angel to the person being prayed for to bring peace in that person's realm.

Angelic Ranks

Angels are organized in ranks, military style. Some angels do better than others in their posts and in the outplay of their duties.

As the saint petitions Heaven bonds for the Bond Registry, an additional understanding of what is being done from the ranks of Heaven's angels will help people understand that they are commanding angels by the courtroom work. This happens through the request for and release of Godly bonds for individuals, entities, and such. This *helps the saint gain a new level of expectation for the playing out of that Godly bond.* If they are not seeing it or sensing it, or if they sense no angel is assigned to take care of this, then the saint can request of the Father, in the courtroom, that His best angels would be assigned to the carrying out of these released bonds.

Released Bonds

Think of these released bonds in a dimensional manner. They are words on a page in a Bond Registry but are also scrolls handed to the Bond Registry Angels. Personal Angels, such as yours, can interact with these angels, offering them backup, support, and assistance.

Individuals have Personal Angels or Guardian Angels, and you can instruct your Personal or Guardian Angel to receive from or to help the Bond Registry Angels. Also, commission your angel(s) to cooperate with the Bond Registry Angels.

For example:

I call the angels assigned to me to come near.

I commission you to cooperate and coordinate with the Bond Registry Angels to fulfill the will of the Father through the release of the Godly bonds placed upon my life, in Jesus' name.

I commission the Bond Registry Angels to cooperate and work with the angels assigned to me, in Jesus' name.

If you're praying for Joe, and you are requesting the release of bonds for Joe, then you can say to Joe's angel, "Do your work with the Bond Registry Angels to receive what they are bringing for Joe." This is a means of commanding angels. You do not have to do this all the time. It can be done in a revelatory manner—in other words, as you perceive, sense, know, see, hear, or have instruction that a Bond Registry Angel needs help, that's when you would request of the Father that Joe's angel would work with the Bond Registry Angel.

Assisting Another's Angel

If someone else's angel comes to you, the chances are that angel is on assignment because they are looking for the saints who can help them. They desire relationship with the saint and, if they do not have one yet with their person, they are hungrily searching for those that they can have relationship with. These angels may need something or need a direction, a commission, or a charge. They may come to you because they know you are sensitive to that and understand these things. Commissioning and charging are also words for commanding angels. The stirring up or calling to attention another person's Personal Angel to their duty has been given to us. This is not outside our boundary. We have the ability to do that.

The Bond Registry

The seer began seeing a book that looked like a Bond Registry. From the Bond Registry, she saw pathways of light extending from the inside pages of the registry. These pathways of light were the angel trails, like a light beam. They were the paths of the Bond Registry Angels on assignment to deliver the bond to the person.

[If you have yet to become acquainted with your personal angels, schedule a Personal Advocacy Session with our team and let us assist you.]

The angel bringing the bond operates to bring what is written on the scroll to the person.

---

*When someone asks
for the release of a bond,
and that person goes to the court,
follows the protocol, and requests
the release of a particular bond,
that bond gets registered.*

The Angels of the Bond Registry are then released to the realm of that person. If the person who originally asked for someone to request a bond for them is sensitive and perceiving, they will sense the recipient's Personal Angel receive the angel of the registry and bring what the bond releases into their realm. It is a perceivable thing. Some of you have sensed that change. It is discernible. It is a spiritual change and the result of angelic activity of both the Personal Angel and the Angel of the Bond Registry bringing the bond. It often will be written on a scroll. If you sense a delay, you can ask for the Personal Angel to be given backup to receive the Bond Registry Angel.

In some cases, Personal Angels are not practiced at receiving the Bond Registry Angel, so they may need instruction or angelic backup to become experienced with receiving the Bond Registry Angel.

In the case of a child, the Guardian Angel may need the help of the adult's angel to receive the Bond Registry Angel and learn this type of angelic duty.

Be sensitive to engage these angels and commission your angel(s) to cooperate with the Bond Registry Angels to fulfill what is in your scroll.

Chapter 12
Bonds in Governmental Intercession

While meeting with a small intercessory group where I live, I taught on the principle of spiritual bonds. Following the teaching, we began to exercise what we had learned and applied it to some situations in our county. I will describe a bit of the story as it unfolded.

County-Level Bonds Release

First, we requested access to the Register of Bonds for this particular county. We saw a number of ungodly bonds as well as some Godly ones.

Godly Bonds	Ungodly Bonds
Bond of Love for Christianity	Prejudice
	Ungodly Leadership

After clearing the ungodly bonds, we requested some new Godly bonds. We looked into Heaven to see what was happening, and she could see scrolls being written and handed out to angels for dispatch. Some of the angels were rejoicing and high-fiving one another.

Godly Bonds	Ungodly Bonds
Bond of Love for Christianity	~~Prejudice~~
Bond of Integrity in Leadership	~~Ungodly Leadership~~
Bond of Love	
Bond of Clarity	

Following the release of these bonds, we requested access to the Court of Decrees and requested to see the map to find out where we needed to have booby traps set. The indications were to have them set on the entry points into the county, so we made the request in the Court of Decrees and saw angels setting the booby traps as we had requested.

Following this, we asked to look at the registry for the County Commissioners and began working on that arena. Remember, the County Commissioners are a group, so they will have a registry. Any recognized group will have a registry. Because we have a vested interest in this county and we pay taxes into it, we have permission to responsibly look into this information.

As the seer looked, she could not see clearly what was on the page. At that point, I began repentance for every ungodly trade the commissioners had been involved in. We forgave, blessed, and released them and requested release from the consequences of their actions. We requested some Godly bonds be released, which were empty before. The bonds in the right column were listed and were dealt with via a Writ of Severance.

Godly Bonds	Ungodly Bonds
Bond of Openness in Government	~~Bond of Cloaking~~
Bond of Clarity	~~Bond of Fraud~~
Bond of Fairness	
Bond of Genuineness	
Cooperation	
Bond of Release of the Might & Power of God	
Sincerity	

Once we felt a release from this part, we then looked into the school board. Again, we pay taxes to the county, and the school board is a recipient. How well they do directly affects my life as a citizen of the county.

Godly Bonds	Ungodly Bonds
	Injustice
	Fear
	Unconcern
	Disengagement
	Detachment
	Separation

Nothing was in the left column. At this point, it was not a surprise because the revelation of bonds was only weeks old.

We began obtaining Writs of Severance from the ungodly bonds we had discovered. Then we dealt with the consequences of the bonds in the Court of Cancellations and requested restitution.

We then returned to the Court of Titles and Deeds and requested the following Godly bonds.

Godly Bonds	Ungodly Bonds
Justice	~~Injustice~~
Love	~~Fear~~
Clarity in how to properly operate the school system	~~Unconcern~~
Clarity—Writ of Release of the Might and Power of God	~~Disengagement~~
Concern	~~Detachment~~
Engagement	~~Separation~~
Peace	
Unity	

Governmental Level Bonds Release

I met with another group the following day, and we followed the same pattern. The results were immediate, and the degree of release was felt by everyone participating.

Continuing to learn about bonds, we engaged Heaven for more insight and asked about intercession for government.

The first tip is not to lean on your own understanding. Remember that Heaven does play a part in the governments of nations with some of its own timeline, its own agenda, and the Father's heart for that nation. So going into the Courts of Heaven to get bonds for governments is going to require a sensitivity to help steer it and a sensitivity to those in the court who know things and can contribute to our request for a bond for a government of a nation.

Gaining Counsel

We could request that one who does have an assignment to that nation join us in the Court of Titles and Deeds to give counsel regarding the type of bond to request. We would simply call their spirit to the Court to counsel with us.

The citizens of Heaven are going to want to give input and counsel. They want to trade into the bond if they are given a chance so that you have the church in Heaven and the church on Earth operating in tandem.

Sometimes, in the requesting of bonds, we are not giving time for Heaven to summon those into the court who have understanding about the types of bonds they could utilize. They could be given room, and we could hear from them about the types and breadths of the bonds that we are asking for governments and for governments of nations.

If we do it this way—inviting others into the Court of Titles and Deeds and requesting their counsel on a bond request for a government, it might be quite shocking what we hear because it may go against our preconceived notions and ideas of what we are requesting for a particular government of a nation or government of a society.

Once again, it is always good to request bonds, as they are wonderful things to request from Heaven, employing resources that we know not of, but by faith achieve.

It is possible for those who can see in the spirit realm to how these bonds are affecting that group once they have been applied. For those seeing in the spirit, when the bonds are being applied (by angels) it looks like raindrops falling over a map of geographical and governmental locations.

For the government of the United States, the council of those in Heaven who would be invited into the Court of Titles and Deeds to help us determine the righteous bond to use, would also have information regarding who that bond really should go to.

For instance, when we think about the United States of America, certain bonds are needed for the church in the beltway of the District of Columbia, as well as in the beltway of the Northern Virginia and Maryland suburbs—in those specific geographical locations. We can know this because often bonds are connected to geographical areas and areas in the natural realm that are not necessarily marked geographies, but they're considered geographies in the spirit.

For instance, we have terms for "those in the beltway," or "those outside the beltway," those "across the tracks," using common terms of speech that we use to refer to groups in cities and in locations. It is like that also for levels of government in terms of national government.

A correlation exists between the type of bonds that we might request, the breadth of those bonds, and to whom we request the bond to go toward, and the work of what we call principalities and powers because they are also geographically anchored. Certain powers of darkness anchored into geography are offset when we request bonds for the church, the unsaved, the national leaders, and the government leaders in an area. And if we get input from Heaven, it's going to give us the very type of bond that empowers those groups greatly, simply because it came from Heaven's information about how that principality was operating in darkness.

Therefore, let's look concerning some of the bonds at the state level. A bond for those inhabitants in the state of California would be different from a bond that we would request in the state of Minnesota. Wouldn't it be great to have input from the heavenly realm in our court session to know what type of bond our specific geographical location would need? This is true for cities and city governments, county and county governments, states, and nations. Even what were once called city-states.

Bonds for Gatekeepers

When we are asking Heaven for its input on how to ask for bonds for governments, we are essentially asking to know what bonds to assign to the gatekeepers[15] of that particular governing body. Whether they know it or not, whether they see it only from the natural realm, or they are able to see it (and some do from the supernatural or the spiritual realm) is that there are groups that operate in both. But asking for a bond for a Godly gate and Godly gatekeeper would empower that gatekeeper to monitor the traffic coming in and out of that gate.

Asking for a bond for a Godly gate and Godly gatekeeper would empower that gatekeeper to monitor the traffic coming in and out of that gate.

This could affect things like the trafficking of humans, the trafficking of souls, and the trafficking of the trade of material and immaterial things. Even the trade out of other realms, which would be immaterial things, would

---

[15] Gatekeeper – a person or entity that controls access to a spiritual realm.

have results in the natural realm that we could see for all these are under the jurisdiction of Heaven and the King. All of these fall under the jurisdiction of the Throne of God. Thus, the sons of God can operate in them when they can open their mind to understand, by the renewing of their mind that realms have gates.

> *Realms have gates.*

The Gatekeeper Anointing

The spiritual realm can easily identify who in the natural realm carries a gatekeeper anointing, a gatekeeper calling, and a gatekeeper positioning. Not all gatekeepers operate knowing this information and some operate with knowing in a haphazard way.

Some are very keen to know their ability as a gatekeeper but often fall into sin, even darkness, and are captured by numerous verdicts from hell's courts—courts of darkness that began to utilize that gatekeeper for their evil. Largely the church has been ignorant of this, while some churches have been established in certain geographical locations because they do have a gatekeeper. There is a gatekeeper anointing and gatekeeper calling, but since most churches are clueless about it, illegitimate gates are often opened and at work.

> *The sleeping church must be awakened.*

Gatekeepers can be individuals, or they can be groups. Gatekeepers are often like-minded in the pursuit of discerning access to their area of focus. Like a harbor master knows what comes and what goes, he is not really in charge of what, when, and where things travel through, but mostly he's just paying attention and logging it. However, he has a mandate for certain things that he knows cannot come through his harbor, so he disallows them. That is just gate management, but the sons of God have the authority from Heaven for the places by which they can conduct the management of the Gates.

The sons of God have the authority
from Heaven for the places
in their jurisdiction
by which they can conduct
the management of the Gates.

In Scripture, we are told to pray for those in authority. Gatekeepers are positioned in places of authority, whether they are individuals or whether they are groups of people. An example of groups would be churches. These gatekeepers seem to have both regional jurisdiction like where we can see a large gate and we can see smaller gates. They all operate as gatekeepers. The different groups and different individuals would have varying degrees of authority in their gate. When praying for those in authority, we are praying for the issuance of bonds. Consider: For instance, we might request a Bond of Disallowance, a Bond of Clarity, a Bond of Supernatural Awareness, and a Bond of Spiritual Sensitivity.

This would manifest in the physical where the individual or the group of believers would have a physical manifestation within their body notifying them that they need to make a management activity or a judgment activity in their gate. They could feel this. They could sense it.

Angels are assigned to gatekeepers.

This is because angels are assigned to gatekeepers, and one of their jobs is to help the gatekeeper understand his role even to the point of the timing when they may be distracted by something going on in the supernatural realm, the angel's job is to help alert that gatekeeper.

Gatekeepers can also lock arms in the spirit.

This would be different gatekeepers, both what we would describe as vertical, but also as horizontal, where differing groups of gatekeepers would get together and disallow or manage their gates in tandem. Vertical gatekeepers guard access from a second heaven to the earth perspective, whereas horizontal gatekeepers control access on what would desire access around them to their left, right, front or behind.

For that to happen, you need Bonds of Agreement, Bonds of Unity of the Brethren, Bonds of Love One for Another, Bonds of Love for the Church, and even a Bond of Awakening. This is regarding the gatekeepers within the Body of Christ because they would know their positioning; they would know their authority and the groups' authority, too. Some are already aware of their authority this way and have made moves to join in league with others. Also, we should request a Bond of Knowledge for a gatekeeper or a group.

As we continue to learn more about the application of these understandings, may the governments of our land rise to new levels of integrity and positive influence as they become God-honoring institutions, blessing the people whom they serve. Other suggestions concerning governmental intercession and the use of bonds are in the Q&A's later in this book. May you avail yourself of this powerful tool to advance the Kingdom of Heaven.

More insights on governmental intercession and procedures are covered in *Engaging the Courts for Your City*[16] as well as *Dealing with Trusts & Consequential Liens in the Courts of Heaven*.

---

[16] LifeSpring Publishing, 2019.

Chapter 13

Sources of Ungodly Bonds

As the seer and I worked through the ministry's Bond Registry, we learned that sometimes additional columns would be opened to us. One of these was the "Date of Entry" column, which gave a timeframe of when that particular bond was placed on the registry. This can be helpful information to know how long a bond has been on the registry.

The other column we occasionally were allowed to see was the "Source of the Bond" column. This allowed us to know if the bond was placed by a court of hell, the counsels of hell, a human, or by witches or some similar source. Often, ungodly bonds are placed by a court of hell or a counsel of hell. At other times, a human may be involved in placing ungodly bonds. We have had to get ungodly bonds removed from clients or donors to the ministry. For example, in our ministry, if a client is disgruntled with their Personal Advocacy Session, their complaint will easily be met with agreement by the enemy and an ungodly bond will be placed upon the

Bond Registry of the ministry. This has happened more than once. Please be cognizant of your complaints against someone or against a ministry. It is creating unnecessary hindrances.

On one occasion, someone ordered one of our books around 4:55 on a Friday afternoon. When an order is placed for a PDF version of a product, the ordering process automatically forwards the person to the link to download the PDF document. Our system worked fine, but the customer overlooked the link and decided we had not fulfilled the order. A few minutes after 5:00 PM that day, she called our office. On Fridays, we typically close by 5:00 PM, so no one was available to respond to her. Since we did not respond to her call, she immediately filed a complaint with PayPal, saying we did not fulfill our end of the bargain, which began an entire series of aggravations for our staff when we came into the office on Monday morning. All because of the client's impatience.

We ended up with ungodly bonds on our Bond Registry, plus we also had to satisfy the complaint with PayPal, which took quite a bit of time. This one instance was quite troublesome for our team to deal with, and was entirely unnecessary. We would have easily handled the matter had we been given a little time to do so. We have a very small administrative staff to handle things like this.

On another occasion, I was impressed to check the Bond Registry of the ministry. An ungodly bond was listed, and when I inquired about the source, it said, "Competing Ministry." I thought that was an interesting way to put it. We did not know who the "competing ministry" was, but we dealt with the ungodly bond and cleared it.

Later that day, I again felt impressed to check the Bond Registry, and to my surprise, I found the same bond listed again; this time, the source again said, "Competing Ministry," but when we inquired, we were informed that it was a different competing ministry. We forgave, blessed, released them, and got the bond removed from our registry for the second time. It was the same ungodly bond on the same day but from a different source.

Once again, later that afternoon, I was again impressed to check the Bond Registry, and lo and behold, I saw the same bond listed as before, but a different "Competing Ministry." This was rather uncanny. We forgave, blessed, and released the party involved but were curious as to why we had to deal with it three times in one day.

Apparently, the enemy did not like what we were doing and wanted to harass us. We don't view ourselves as competing with anyone. We do what we do. Others do what they do. It is not like we have a shortage of hurting people to minister to because we certainly do not. I also understand that the Father is not setting up Courts of Heaven franchises where we have exclusive dibs on the Courts of Heaven. It is the Courts of Heaven, not the

Courts of Ron or anyone else. We are privileged to have access to the Courts of Heaven and are grateful for it.

We must realize that our jealousies and immature actions can cause others much aggravation and consternation. If you have aught against someone, rest assured that Satan is all too happy to agree with you and get ungodly bonds placed against someone to appease your grievance. We must grow up in these things. The extension of the Kingdom is too important to deal with petty issues and jealousy.

You will experience times when Heaven does not allow you to read the source column. For one, it is often easier NOT to know who initiated the ungodly bond. If it was someone you knew, it might make your relationship with them more difficult. Simply forgive, bless, and release the perpetrators and move on. Don't waste time on petty matters.

To think that all ungodly bonds arise from the courts or councils of hell would be nice and simplistic. However, that is not always the case. While there are councils of hell that meet to collaborate and develop strategies against the saints, they are not the only ones that are developing strategies to impact our lives. We need to consider the work of witches and other workers of darkness, specific demons, covens, non-believers, and yes, even saints.

We engaged with Heaven to learn some of these things where this information was unveiled.

We asked to see the Bond Registry for LifeSpring, mainly to see the ungodly bonds. The first on the list was an ungodly Bond of Heresy. The next was a Bond of Lengthening—as in "going outside our parameters." It gives the feeling that one is illegally lengthening their stride. We saw a Bond of a Closed Door set to prevent us from opening new doors. Next was a Bond of Wandering and a Bond of Carelessness.

The first bond we saw was a Bond of Heresy. Not everyone agrees with what we teach, and that is fine. We are not presenting what we teach as doctrine but as revelation as revealed to us. Revelation is often simply a new way of approaching an old truth—a new way of seeing an old truth or a different explanation. Sometimes it is something hidden in the Word of God that has simply been unveiled.

When people fear deception, they often end up being deceived because, inadvertently, they have come into agreement with fear. Those that are familiar with our ministry often hear me say,

> *We will not agree with fear,*
> *on any level, at any time,*
> *about anything.*

> *Agreeing with fear is agreeing*
> *with councils of darkness.*

The source of this first ungodly bond was **members of the bride agreeing or operating from fear.** When we agree with fear, councils of darkness will gladly come alongside and work with someone to establish the ungodly bond. Then, the Court of Accusation (a court of hell) will work to establish the ungodly bond.

The next bond, the Bond of Lengthening, is like a complaint **from other believers who felt the ministry was lengthening its stride too much.** We were gaining too much momentum for their liking, so they put the Bond of Lengthening on our registry.

The Bond of a Closed Door was simply **from the court of hell.** On another occasion we detected an ungodly Bond of Growing Too Fast, and on the same page was an ungodly Bond of Not Growing Fast Enough. All from the courts of hell. Which is it, hell? Too fast or not fast enough? Sometimes the bonds do not make sense.

The Bond of Wandering that was detected had the feel of a witchcraft spell—like a ritual spell. **The source of it was witchcraft.**

Another was a Bond of Shoddy Work. This one came from **the complaint of one of our clients** where we did not meet her expectations of how we do things, and finally, a Bond of Carelessness. It too was **from a client's complaint.**

As a ministry, we endeavor to do our best to serve clients; however, many variables are involved in making that happen. We sometimes have issues with suppliers, software, and computers, misunderstandings, and communication issues. We serve hundreds of clients yearly, and a lot can happen during that time.

We work to resolve every issue positively, but that cannot always happen as we are dealing with people and their expectations. We do our best and forgive, bless, and release as needed.

Ignorant or Intentional Placement

Sometimes, we want to tell people they don't know what they are doing when they complain about someone to another person, or in their prayer time, but that is not always the case. Some people—whether believers or not, know exactly what they are doing. Mercy is a lot easier for someone acting out of ignorance but a little more challenging to offer to someone who intentionally lodges a complaint in the spirit against someone or a ministry.

With a couple of complaints coming from the disgruntled client, we knew who the client was. However, it is not always best to know who placed the ungodly bond as our soul may have trouble dealing with the situation. Sometimes knowing who was responsible makes it harder to walk in and extend forgiveness to them. Often that information will be hidden from you for your benefit.

For a believer to knowingly place ungodly bonds on your Bond Registry is a form of manipulation and what we often call "charismatic witchcraft." We must walk in forgiveness regardless.

We always want to be aware that our complaints create more than just accusations or false verdicts; they can create ungodly bonds. We should always have a sensitivity of heart that notifies us when we cross the line. Then, we need to quickly repent and request the removal of the ungodly bond, false verdict, or accusation that we have been responsible for placing.

When we realize how these ungodly bonds are formed and how critical it is that we are not responsible for doing so because the enemy is using our words of complaint, discontent, anger, and derision to manipulate situations and people to do the bidding of workers of darkness and councils of hell. The voice of the bride needs both education and discipline, and this begins with knowledge. That is why we are using our experience to help others understand the depth of their chosen words and how these operate behind the scenes and are placed in bond registries.

The seer and I noticed soberness in the court as the Just Judge began talking to me about the wickedness of evil and how evil will use even this knowledge of bonds because when you have the knowledge, you are called to a higher, stricter place of discipline. Simply because you've been given this knowledge and understanding and it resonates in you as you release godly bonds, the discipline of it is the necessary schooling of your mouth not to agree with hell in the issuance of ungodly bonds.

There is a correlation between your knowledge of this information—this revelation, and Satan's ear too. He uses it against you because you know more about releasing ungodly bonds. Then, he's ever keener to listen to you and to use your mouth against you, and he has legal ground and right to do that because he sees your understanding of the other side—the good side of it.

Therefore, he has some legal ground with deeper accusations against you because you have reached a greater plane of understanding and are being disciplined as a son. Therefore, when you complain, he comes to accuse you at a higher level because of the knowledge that you've received. It's a form of growing up and paying attention to the nuances of how evil will want to work against your life. God's children have need of this plain speech to become aware of the enemy's plots against them and those moving in this revelation. The Father's desire is not for them to fall into a pit or to lead others astray inadvertently simply because they carry this revelation.

Following this information about the ungodly bonds, we then began the work for their removal:

> *Father, we ask permission to enter Your Court of Titles and Deeds in Jesus' name. We are here on behalf of LifeSpring International Ministries, and we request of this court a Writ of Severance for the Ungodly Bond of Heresy, the Ungodly Bond of Lengthening, the Ungodly Bond of Closed Door, the Ungodly Bond of Wandering, the Ungodly*

Bond of Shoddy Work, and the Ungodly Bond of Carelessness.

[Pause to receive the verdicts]

Father, I ask to enter into the Court of Cancellations in the name of Jesus. Our request is to have these Writs of Severance entered this court. We request the full cancellation of the Ungodly Bond of Heresy against LifeSpring International Ministries. We ask for the full cancellation of the Ungodly Bond of Lengthening, Closed Doors, Wandering, Shoddy Work, and Carelessness.

We request the full cancellation of each of these bonds, all of their ramifications, all of their impact against LifeSpring International Ministries, and where LifeSpring International Ministries has been stolen from or has suffered, we request restitution.

We release forgiveness to <u>name of party</u> in the name of Jesus. We choose to release them. We choose to forgive them, and we choose to bless them in Jesus' name.

We ask for an amendment against the witchcraft operating against the ministry. We ask for an amendment that they would know the glory of God, and that they would be given opportunity to repent, and if not repenting, we request a gag order against them where their operation is against LifeSpring International Ministries.

We also choose to forgive in this court those members of the Bride operating from fear, which has brought the heresy charge—the heresy bond into being. We forgive them, bless them, and release them in the name of Jesus.

As we waited for the verdicts from our request, the court suggested that we request of the court for those members of the bride who are in fear to be set free from fear—set free from the fear they have agreed with about this ministry.

Thank you, Father, for these cancellations.

We received the necessary verdicts and then set about requesting some Godly Bonds on our behalf.

The Release of Fiery Arrows

As part of the same engagement, we were instructed to deal with ungodly bonds coming from workers, darkness and councils of hell. The Father is never outdone by the works of darkness or the deeds of the workers of darkness. Our focus is not on the works of darkness but on the one who is the true light giver—Jesus, the light of the world.

It's always good to glorify God in the presence of darkness.

The Father is delighted that we would do this as an authentic move against the working of evil. He wished more people were doing this.

A new strategy he added to our toolbelt was to access the Court of Cancellations and request an Amendment for the Release of the Fire of God against the worker(s) of darkness responsible (including the council of hell).

When we see things on the ungodly bond registries, it is always good to take the next step—the offensive step to release the weapons of God's warfare against the enemy.

This is not the same as plundering the enemy. It is almost like making a declaration of the glory of God. Hell, already knows it, but Heaven loves to enforce it.

We call this "in your face."

Chapter 14
Trading on Ungodly Bonds

A current global crisis was on our minds when Eric (a man in white who was tutoring us) came to give us instruction.

The realm of darkness is engaged in ungodly bonds, and they are trading on them. Some ungodly bonds come from the soulish actions of people, others from the courts of hell, and still others from galactic interference.[17]

Imagine an entity—a galactic being[18]—trading on the power of how many ungodly bonds they have released against the sons of God. They do not receive power directly from the person they have put the bond on but rather from the activity of placing the bond itself. That ungodly realm educates and rewards them for placing ungodly bonds on men. They learn by searching out the

---

[17] Galactic refers to planets and systems outside our own.

[18] Heaven has been broadening our understanding about interdimensional races of beings that we previously weren't aware of that are, as yet, unredeemed.

counsels of hell and the legalities of the process for working in darkness. The bond can come from the bloodline of the saint, and the galactic entity works to find iniquities in the bloodline and then place the ungodly bond on that person in the courts of hell. These galactic entities are recognized for however many ungodly bonds are successfully applied and they gain power by doing this.

This makes the courtrooms of Heaven revelation imperative for the sons of God to realize that they have access to remove the legal grounds, because the enemy is using them against the saints. That realm can recognize those who have studied and found loopholes and devious ways to trip the saints up so they can bring charges and have legal grounds to then implant an ungodly bond.

The power these unredeemed galactic entities gain isn't stolen from the saint assigned the ungodly bond, it comes from darkness and the power comes in proportion to how many people the ungodly bond affects.

Let's say we have a person in India and an ungodly bond is loosed against him, his community, and all the places his life touches. To afflict a man who has lots of sway in a community would grant the entity more power. The more influence the recipient has, the more power is derived from placing the ungodly bond. This would incentivize these beings for tripping up major leaders in the Body of Christ. That power could be applied and works generationally through several people living on the earth. Let's say we have a person in

India and an ungodly bond is loosed against a man, his community, and however many places that his life touches (which is going to exponentially increase)—to afflict a man who has a lot of sway in a community would grant the being more power. The more influence the recipient has, the more power is derived from placing the ungodly bond. It would be important to trip up a major leader in the Body of Christ.

A person's sphere of influence, their following and even their family lines are involved. Imagine Celebrity A marries Celebrity B, and the influence of that one celebrity to the other cross-germinates so the influence is multiplied. The entities would be rewarded more for taking down this couple with ungodly bonds. Because, their fall or trip-up would influence so many more people for darkness.

Height and width were mentioned, and we wondered what that meant. It was explained to us as the height of a person's status and the width of their reach—but do not let that confuse us that the councils of hell are not also searching out the grandmother who prays in her house constantly and has little influence or power—they work to stop both.

Imagine a grandmother like that praying in her living room but operating in the courts to remove the bonds, from herself and others—what a powerhouse she is, what a hidden fire she is.

We had a sense that the bonds that were on the galactic level were on a different plane than the bonds we have been dealing with typically.

We have dealt with the demonic principalities and powers, but we occasionally deal with galactic entities or princes. They are the ones responsible for the high-tech tracking devices that are not an average run-of-the-mill tracking device. They have a bond that goes on a different level. That was the inference to us. We had been coming across that often. This would fall into the category of other realms—bonds from other realms. This is the essence of the dirty trade, and the other realm beings are interested in working with spirits assigned against the earth. The galactic beings do not want to get their hands dirty, so they work like hidden slave masters behind the curtain and employ others to do the work for them. My sense of this is these beings are separate from our low-level demons, but they feel more intelligent. We have our low-level demon who works for a boss, right? And then that boss works for a boss, correct? Those are all earthbound earth realm evil beings, but the beings behind the curtain are these galactic beings that employ the bosses that work the demons as slaves—it is like that.

The intensity level of the evil here is increased exponentially. It is vastly increased, and these evil beings have divided themselves into leagues. There is great competition among these leagues to gain influence and power in the running of the evil realm and the evil spirits/low-level demons.

Prince Pretenders

For instance, a low-level demon manages to trip up a person of profound influence. Then he brings that to the boss, and that boss brings it to his boss. The earth-realm principality boss then takes that to the galactic being. The galactic being, along with his league, is empowered by that trade, which translates to the fact that he now has more status against the other leagues. They are prince pretenders, also known as princes of the power of the air.

We asked about the removal of these bonds—can we do so in the same way, or is there a different location for those records? Heaven told us that we would need greater access for that, so we asked if it would require a key or a badge or if we could request access. We were told it was a matter of timing. If we run into this when doing bond work, just keep doing the bond severance the way we have been taught.

The bond severance that we have been taught—the spread of it and the use of it by the saints, especially the use of it over cities—is so young still that it needs time to grow. We must have more embracing of this revelation by the saints. We must have more engagement in the severance of bonds. Remember individual, family, city, nations—it must mushroom. It must grow. It must be seeded into the earthly realm. As we do that, the gained power of these prince pretenders and the power they have been given is redeemed. There will come a day when the next level of bond severance is open to the saints, but that has not happened yet.[19]

Do not think it's linear; work so that we are approved as good workmen and can continue in the task until that day.

Transition of Trade

In a vision, a giant ship could be seen, and we understood that the ship represented a trade route. In the vision, the ship was Phoenician. We were seeing it because what we are undergoing in the current day is a transition of trade. Due to Coronavirus, the earth's populations have been under duress, a transition of trade. For some it has been a positive trade, but for most it was a negative trade.

A person in white, whose name we were not given, came forth and explained that he operates in the merchant area of the Business Complex. He explained that the ship was in reference to transition of trade.

Nations are created to trade. Their population within the nations itself is created to trade on many levels of trading. The unseen realm works through trade as well. The profaning of trade is sin. When we profane trade at certain levels, it corrupts purpose and destiny. For

---

[19] At the time we received this revelation, the information covered in *Dealing with Trusts & Consequential Liens in the Courts of Heaven* had not been unveiled.

example, the spreading of the gospel through local churches was hindered by the restrictions placed up on churches to not meet. These churches' purpose and destiny was affected. Some experienced great loss during this time. Some simply were unable to survive the rough spot of the shutdowns. Trade routes are being traded in galactic areas right now. Entities are competing to for the power gained when they corrupt God's purpose and destiny for mankind.

The trade routes themselves are up for auction in the earth, which is why the earth is experiencing this duress. We were told that Coronavirus is being used as a tool to implement this transition of trade. This is against the will of the Father and outside of the timing of Heaven. Satan is trying to change times and seasons.

Trade routes and all their many dimensions are synchronized with the time of the Lord, like in the days of Nebuchadnezzar. Nebuchadnezzar had reached a pinnacle point in the control of trade, which began to corrupt him and for which he paid dearly. This was related to Babylon—it was premature. Nebuchadnezzar was like a pawn to galactic entities trying to make trade route changes that the Father had not approved.

We would have to look between the lines to see this in Scripture, but it is there. Remember the statue that Daniel saw. Each of those time markers was another attempt at violating trade routes, and they are trading off their bluffing. They often bluff like in poker. It is dishonest trading. These beings will use humans or demonic spirits. They will use the interplay of their spirit when one person says, "I have this," and the other guy says, "Maybe you do." It is not a pleasant, honest activity that they hope to engage in one day. These beings will use humans or spirits. They will use the interplay of their spirit realm society's maneuverings. They have been doing this since ancient times.

---
*Their goal is the earth
and to dominate humanity.*

Chapter 15

Two New Bonds

This chapter is from a blog post written at the beginning of January 2021 on our website[20] about two new bonds we learned of.

The Bond of Filtering
& The Bond of Undoing

On this day, we engaged Heaven, and they were concerned for one of our team members, a New York state resident. They gave us the following instructions that will be beneficial to you. For this article, I will refer to him as Jesse. Here was Heaven's instruction:

"Jesse needs a thing called 'undoing.' It is like quieting. It is an activity of angels.

---

[20] www.courtsofheavenwebinars.com

"Think of where Jesse lives; he is in the state of New York. New York is under some principality thrones and some witchcraft—Jezebel witchcraft. The state of New York is under a Jezebel witchcraft spell. The realms of those who carry the Father's light feel the resistance in the spirit realm to their light.

Writ of Undoing

"Undoing is a work of angelic hosts to undo spells of witchcraft. When you become aware of a witchcraft activity through human agents and the voices of those aligned with darkness, angels can be requested to operate. You can ask this as an amendment to a court case or you can appear in the Court of Angels to request a Writ of Undoing. It is easier for angels to operate undoing through paperwork from other court cases, and you can ask of the Father that the angels carry out this Writ of Undoing.

"Do not play with this one. This is not something to be done on a whim. Only do this <u>when you have been told to,</u> and you are assured that witchcraft is in play. The human soul cannot lead you to the accuracy of this discernment. You will need to discern it *by the spirit.*

Bond of Undoing

"If you see witchcraft bonds in the Bond Registry, you can request a Godly Bond of Undoing. It is a bond at that point. That bond on the Bond Registry releases the paperwork to angels to carry out the undoing. It is immensely powerful. You can use it as a defense item and as often as necessary, but let me be clear. <u>Do not</u> guess at this!

Bond of Filtering

"I want to tell you about another bond. It is called the Bond of Filtering. This bond also releases powerful paperwork to angels on behalf of the individual; a Bond of Filtering will help your physical atmosphere so that your spirit is more able to discern spiritual things. You may have to work with this one for a while to realize how it works. A Bond of Filtering is for angelic activity in that person's atmosphere to cause discernment and revelation at a higher level. It enables the atmosphere to carry spiritual discernment and knowing at a higher upgraded level.

"These bonds are often found together or are good to use hand-in-hand because they can work in tandem. When you have been told that witchcraft is at play, you need the Bond of Undoing. You can also subsequently ask for the Bond of Filtering, as that causes filtering in the spirit that angels are helping with so that the human spirit is catching, grasping, and knowing—all these phrases, meaning they become more aware of what is happening. A mature saint operating under the Bond of Filtering then is enabled and empowered to be their spiritual self with their spirit forward and operate from that route from the Father's realm. This may also help with their dreaming during their night seasons."

With one more question, our engagement was over. "This is when you expose the enemy's work so that you can employ the use of the angelic host?" we asked.

"Yes," Heaven replied with no further explanation.

We have learned that if Heaven doesn't explain something to you that day, they probably will in the future. Simply be listening for it.

May this understanding broaden your work in the realms of Heaven as we see captives set free!

———·———

Chapter 16
Q & A Time

We returned a following day for another class session. This class took the form of a Question and Answer session. Our tutors, Erik and Mark, very graciously answered our questions. Sometimes they chuckled at us and at how quickly or slowly we understood, but we were grateful for the opportunity. In this chapter, we put forth the questions as they came. Some of the information can be added to what was already taught in other parts of the book. I am opting for this format because I am under specific instructions to get the book relased quickly.[21]

Our first question was in response to questions we had received at our office.

---

[21] This refers to the urge from Heaven to make the initial edition of the book available quickly in early 2020, which we were able to do.

When we request a bond for a person or group, does it negate things like accusations against them?

It sort of does. In the case of an individual, a Bond of Clarity would affect a struggle with doublemindedness. The struggle would be pushed back, and sudden moments of clarity would be granted to the individual.

Likewise, with a group (i.e., college students on a campus), issuing a bond out of the resources of Heaven would remove the effect of the negative schemes of the enemy, essentially pushing them back and giving them room for a new thought paradigm.

In the case of a college campus where you ask for a Bond of Grace, space is given for a new thought about how they could appreciate the grace of God in their life. It is not negating the enemy's activity, but it is imparting a sudden strength in the area of specificity of the requested bond.

Specifically with accusations, we were told the removal of the accusations is not met. The bond doesn't meet the accusation. The accusation still must be dealt with.

The bond may affect their ability to get to a place to understand and have it dealt with but doesn't deal with the accusation itself. Accusations stand until dealt with.

Is it the same with false verdicts?

In the case of false verdicts, the individual is highlighted to Heaven for being on a fast track for getting the false verdict removed, but it doesn't remove it. However, depending on the type of bond asked for, it aids the individual's life in such a way as to contribute to the resolution of the false verdict. Once again, the false verdict would stand.

Is it the same pattern concerning covenants or oaths?

Yes, it's the same pattern. A bond enables a person, and it may bring them to a point of decision, helping them see or understand when they have not begun to think, feel, or see that direction. A bond, depending on its specificity and type, would enable that person to gain sight of the covenant or oath they made or that had been made in their bloodline.

If you see an ungodly bond in the registry of bonds that you obtain a writ of severance for, is it necessary to get a counteracting bond on behalf of the person or group?

It's always good to release a Godly bond. Never will you see a time you wouldn't want to release a Godly bond for someone. If you don't know at that moment what bond to put into place, it would be OK not to put one. Unction of Holy Spirit might later bring the specificity of the bond through love for that individual to you, or He might enact that through another who has a broader understanding of that person's life and a deeper love for them. It's always good to establish a bond in a person's life out of Heaven's resources which are so grandly available, but it is not a necessity or a necessary step. It is necessary, however, once seeing a bond that is ungodly in a person's registry, to do all means to remove it as it is working against their life, calling, often their purpose, and even seeking to shut down gifts the Father has granted.

Is our format OK that we are using and teaching in the Court of Cancellations?

Yes, always receive the Writ of Severance. It's always great for the individual to understand the magnitude of the Writ of Severance. A pause might be recommended in a ministry session so the person can sense, feel, or get in touch with the freedom that was just given through the Writ of Severance.

Is there any further recording of that writ that we need to be involved with?

No, it's already taken care of. The Bonds Department takes care of it.

In the Bond Registry, some bonds were highlighted while others were not, which was important. It

seemed to indicate that they were active or inactive. Can you explain that to us?

The ones highlighted or bold are active. The ungodly ones not highlighted or bold are inactive and lack demonic activity at that time. For example, A Bond of Iniquity to a bloodline that seems pale or inactive may be due to evil's lack of attention to that bond, yet it could become active again at any moment. This is often the case with individuals and reflects the activity of evil, specifically with so many witches coming against individuals loosing ungodly bonds in our day.

Groups

When it comes to relationships in groups (a church, for example), if you deal with the bond against that group, does it free the entire group?

The groups must be connected (they have had to agree to be a group) to dismantle an ungodly bond against them. You will use the same procedure as for individuals.

When you obtain a Writ of Severance on behalf of a group, does it release the group as a whole?

Yes, it does for those who agree with the group. The ungodly bond may not affect the people on the fringes of the group who have not made the full agreement in their hearts to be part of that group. In the same manner, the

Writ of Severance would not impact them because they are not a part of the group.

Removing a Bond From a Group

When you remove the bond from a group, do it for the group that agrees. The ungodly bond would not affect those around the group who are not in agreement with the group. They are essentially sightseers. Heaven and hell can tell the difference.

Is there more you would bring to teach us today?

With this question, our tutors began to teach us about releasing bonds for nations. A bond for a nation is connected to time and the cycles and seasons of the Father. Sometimes these are things only the Father knows. All bonds for nations are surrendered to that.

Factions exist within nations, and we can release Godly bonds to a part of a nation—a faction or commonality of a nation—this would be helpful.

Erik gave an example of a current issue in the United States. He told us we could ask for a bond for a particular segment. He cautioned us to be sure to have the Father's heart in our bond request (otherwise, it could become an ungodly bond). We asked for a suggestion of what to ask for, and he suggested a Bond of Awakening. Be sure to have the Father's heart for this. It must be done from love. Note: By the time you see this book, that bond has been requested by me and my team for that segment of our nation.

What about our President?

We were advised to request a Bond of Clarity and a Bond of the Nearness of the Presence for our president. They said President Trump[22] is new in understanding his nearness to God and God's nearness to him, and his level of feeling alone is often heightened.

What about dealing with the impeachment situation?

Our teacher recommended a bond for the Senate as a group. He said it would be better to release a bond over the group than over individuals. He suggested a Bond of Clarity and a Bond of Distinction (highlighting the distinctions Yahweh would point them to). "The Bond of Distinction is very supernatural," we were told.

About a recent current event, Erik offered a real-time suggestion regarding Australia and the recent fires that devastated parts of the country. He suggested we release a Bond of Security—especially to the saints. It brings a wherewithal to know what to do in a crisis because it releases angels with it.

---

[22] Donald Trump was President of the United States at this point in time.

Due to information received just that morning concerning recent policy changes by the government of South Africa, which is affecting whites in South Africa—a Bond of Security is what they also needed.

Remember, always look to love when determining a bond request.

We can ask for bonds for different age segments or groups of a population (Millennials, Generation X, etc.) and subsets of the larger whole.

Seeking Bonds for Nations

The bonds are released to the nation as requested (based on timing) and are collected and weighed on a scale. The bonds begin to pile up. They begin to make a corporate cry—something Heaven is looking into, responding to, and taking note of, mainly because the type of individual who will request a bond for a nation or the faction in a nation has the Father's heart. It is a current and real move of God. All of Heaven is looking at this and counting the number of these types of bonds. The vastness of the quantity of them is going to have a voice in Heaven. This is like the bowls filled with prayer spoken of in Revelation but different. These bonds are being counted in a giant Hall of Justice because it has to do with a nation's justice.

It is like this—as the saints pray for nations and factions within nations and to release bonds, the bonds are counted, and their quantity is recognized in Heaven. So as the nations swing in the balance—as they are judged—all these things are considered by the Father. All of Heaven's resources are now involved in a trade. It will make a difference in what is judged in that Justice Hall concerning that entire nation.

This seems to be connected to very current events—in our recent time frame (as in the last decade and certainly into this new decade).

If we were to release bonds for nations, what nations are at the top of the list?[23]

- Russia
- Ukraine
- China
- Australia
- United Kingdom
- Canada
- Germany

They pointed out that when we have a connection to a nation, that nation is set in our heart in a greater way because we love it because of those we are connected to in it.

---

[23] This was Heaven's priority list in early 2020.

Often, we can look at natural events, earthquakes, volcanoes, etc., to know the priorities of the Lord. These events will move a nation to the top of the list.

Before wrapping it up for that session, we had one final group of questions regarding bonds and the medical arena.

Hospital Information

Emergency Situations

When someone is in an emergency and has been taken to the Emergency Department for care, you often do not have time to go through the standard court protocols to have something taken care of. In the event of someone in an emergency, you can request a bond in their behalf, bypassing the standard protocols.

An Emergency Crisis Bond can be made from the Emergency Department of Heaven's Hospital rather than the other protocol.

We followed up on that information with a question about the Healing Hospital.

Concerning the Healing Hospital, how do bonds work with healing?

Similarly, where they are from the heart of the Father, through love requesting the resources of Heaven for a Bond of Healing, the Bond of Healing can take the form of specificity (not from the healing of the specific disease so much as for the result of wholeness). You could ask for a Bond of Wholeness but make it for a body system (i.e., wholeness for the nervous system, a bond of wholeness for the heart, or for brain activity).

These Bonds of Healing will make it easier for miracles to come forth. For example, if you request a Bond of Healing for someone with brain trauma, the greater the possibility for the miraculous to come forth. This is especially so in this season currently for all body systems because the saints are pressing into miracles. A bond has a connection by easing other intercession for miracles as it concerns healing.

More insights about governmental intercession and breakthrough are available in Volume 2 of this series.

———·———

Chapter 17

Return to Sender

A few months ago, we sent a small package to a customer, expecting it to be delivered in a matter of days. After nearly four months, we were surprised to see the package had been returned to us as undeliverable. After checking the postal service website, we saw our address was correct, but they had deemed it undeliverable. It was stamped "Return to Sender." How many times has that happened to us in the realm of the spirit?

Recently, during an engagement with Heaven, we learned that if I chose to bless someone, and that blessing could not find a landing place in the recipient, then the blessing would return to me, the sender. In that situation, the blessing they would have received is undeliverable because they were unqualified as a recipient due to the state of their heart. I wanted to know how that worked, so I inquired of Heaven the next day. This chapter summarizes what was learned.

The Scripture that a curse causeless shall not alight (Proverbs 26:2) contains the same principle. If no reason exists for a curse to land on someone or something, the curse cannot land. It works that way with curses. If it cannot find a landing place, it is "Returned to Sender."

By the same token, if a blessing can be released to someone but cannot land due to certain sin(s) in that person's life, the blessing returns to the sender, just as a parcel would in our natural world.

Remember that in Luke 6:28, Jesus said to bless those that curse you and pray for them that despitefully use you. To despitefully use someone is to insult, slander, and falsely accuse them. Since the Golden Rule says to do to others as you would have them do unto you, when someone takes it upon themselves to accuse, slander, or insult you falsely, they are stepping in league with the accuser of the brethren. "Your safety in Me," Heaven said, "is that you walk in love with one another."

When you enter accusation, you have stepped out of love and lean toward hatred.

Really, you only have two choices: you either love someone, or you hate them. If you are actively not loving them, you may be demonstrating hatred toward them. That is not a safe place to be.

John the Apostle understood this. He wrote plainly in 1 John 3:8, "He who sins is of the devil." In verse 15, he writes that he who hates his brother is a murderer. If you try to murder someone, either their character or their person, you have stepped out of love and into a place of hatred. Blessing cannot rest in that place.

Therefore, if it cannot land, it must return to the one that sent it. When it returns, it contains the same harvest which was originally sent. If it was a ten-fold harvest when sent, it will be a ten-fold harvest when it lands upon the sender.

At this point, I still had some questions but had to take a break from this engagement with Heaven. Shortly afterward, we re-engaged Heaven for more insights.

We asked Heaven for details regarding a blessing or curse being released and returned to you. What we learned from Heaven is as follows:

If it does not have a cause, it does not alight. This is related to the power of the spoken word, as referred to in the book of James. Words released are living things. Words released *always* have an effect.

A blessing released is a seed that causes an individual to expand.

A curse that is released is a seed that causes the individual to recede or wither. The result of the curse is the withering of that person. The result of a blessing is the expansion of the recipient.

Think of Jesus and the fig tree. The picture of the withering tree was the result of the cursing. It demonstrated the power of God's Word, Jesus, and the swiftness of result—the withering of the fig tree. Notice the swiftness of the result. Curses are designed to bring about a swift result. We can expect the same of a blessing released. A linking exists to the power of life and death in the tongue that needs to be understood.

A curse that cannot alight comes back on the sender.

A curse is not a language of love. It does not come from the Father's Kingdom but is released from the dysfunction of the realms of darkness and the darkened areas within an individual, which are those areas of one's life that have not received enlightenment from the Spirit of God. Both saints and sinners can release curses, but saints should never be so insensitive as to allow their mouths to release curses. Prophetic intercessors must be exceptionally careful with this.

The Curse

Whether the words released are a curse or a blessing, they must land somewhere. They are a type of impartation, and because the Father's heart is to impart blessing and goodness into the lives of individuals, when you release a blessing, it sows itself into a person's realm and has a harvest. This is a principle that God's children are to live by. It is a valuable, beneficial, expansive, glory-initiating, creative act. To release blessing from one's mouth demonstrates the redemption of the tongue through knowing the Savior and the Creator.

When sowed from a place of darkness, this same act of releasing words is released as a curse. It has a similar effect in the opposite direction. It is not the intention of Heaven and certainly not the desire of the Father that one's mouth would be used in this manner.

Where a curse is released, it is seed sown. If the individual or the individual's realm to whom the curse is released is blessed by God, walks with the Lord in all manner of righteousness, does not have a broken wall of defense, and is enjoined by the help of angels, the curse has nowhere to go and comes back to the one who sent it. The sender reaps their misguided release of power. Words, like deeds, are powerful in their creative role and effect on the world.

Since the enemy knows this, he uses the wounded and darkened areas of God's people to do his dirty work to release curses. It does not bother Satan that the individual who releases curses out of immaturity and ignorance would be harmed by their release, as his evil contains no balance for that.

However, for a believer to release curses is not the plan of God for that individual. The redemption of that is the awakened realization that they are engaging in self-cursing if they release a curse against someone walking in righteousness. Thus, we have the Scriptural principle to bless and curse not. My righteousness protects me, and your righteousness protects you. It provides a deflective shield to cause the curses to return to the sender. It is not the Father's heart that you would release curses in league with the enemy of your soul out of your woundedness and brokenness.

It takes a mindset of the Lord and a oneness with His mind to release a blessing in the face of difficult circumstances.

For example, Jesus on the cross, when He requests of the Father that His persecutors would be forgiven for "they know not what they do," is a sincere form of blessing in the face of great obstacles, pain, and hardship.

Since all words are recorded in Heaven, angels pay attention to the saints of God and what is being released from their mouths. Thus, we have the conviction of the Spirit of God within an individual to close their mouth and walk away, as well as the saying in the world, "If you cannot say something nice, do not say anything at all." Would it not be wise to withhold one's tongue from releasing a curse out of the hardship of a circumstance?

This is problematic for maturing saints, primarily because the soul is often in charge of the mouth. In contrast, the believer walking in oneness with God has a sense of Holy Spirit's function to release blessing only and thereby override the soul's tendency to not think in oneness with God.

Quartermaster

Your spirit must act like a quartermaster over your realm to release blessings, not curses. A quartermaster oversees the supplies for a military unit. At your request, the quartermaster of your realm releases blessing on your behalf.

> *The supply of blessing increases as you release blessing.*

Blessings released in the face of great hardship are noted in Heaven because you, in that instance, have become an overcomer against the plot of the enemy, working from the fallen world in conjunction with the strife of the soul. Your spirit operates like a quartermaster, releasing the blessing of the Father to the members of the Bride, to the Army of God, and to the family of Yahweh.

When God's many blessings are seen upon the people of God, it defeats darkness, and it causes friction in those bound in darkness to hunger and desire the blessing of God on His people, His children, and His sons.

> *The abundance of the riches
> of Heaven come from
> the release of verbal blessing.*

Blessing is Not a Sentiment

Do not be mistaken. The release of the blessings in the name of the King accomplishes much in the body and the Bride of Christ that overflows even to the world. Do not be mistaken that a blessing or the release of blessing by your words is a sentiment. It is not a sentiment. It is not an emotion. It is a spirit-bearing release of the Kingdom's pleasure—the good pleasure of the Father from the Kingdom realm of glory with the intent to increase, expand, and cause growth in the brothers and sisters of Jesus.

Focused Blessing

Heaven says focused blessing is best. Just like the enemy uses a focused curse as a tool of bondage, aim your blessing with more specificity and engage the faith within you as you release it. This is powerful.

A good blessing is the blessing to overcome, stating, "I bless you to overcome," followed by the invitation to overcome a specific thing like someone's surgery.

- I bless you to overcome your surgical procedure.

- I bless you to overcome your physical therapy sessions.
- I bless you to overcome pain.
- I bless you to overcome fear.
- I bless you to overcome in every circumstance.

These are true blessings of the Lord. They help us to strengthen and empower one another through expressed hope coupled with firm faith.

It is hope with firmness established in faith.

Another great blessing is the blessing of revelation.

- I bless you for the revealed expression of God in that circumstance.
- I bless you for a revelatory encounter.
- I bless you for a revelation of relationship.
- I bless you for revelation of insight.
- I bless you for revelation of solution.

These are true blessings.

Specific Causes

We asked Heaven, "Are there specific causes for someone to experience the ricochet of a blessing?"

Heaven answered, "All sin should be directed under the Blood of Jesus. The sacrifice of the Lamb of God was given so that the sin would be made null so that the blessing can fall. This is related to your authoritative release to forgive someone of their sin and bless them, for the Father desires to reach their heart. His redemptive work is at play even now in the hearts of the nations. For example, you might release a blessing to someone, which returns to you. Instead of that being the end of the story, forgive the person for their sin that caused the ricochet effect, bless them again, and release them from the hold the sin had upon them. Then re-release the prior blessing to them, and they should be able to receive it this time."

The Body of Christ is awakening to the adequacy of what Jesus took care of. This is quantitatively being released from Heaven in new ways so that the sons of God awaken to their truest destiny as the releasers of redemption.

Jesus was the gift to take care of the sin problem. All those who come to the Father through Him have forgiveness, but it is the continual work of the Holy Spirit to convict a son or daughter of God of their need for forgiveness in areas where they have not walked in perfection. Regardless of what they have done, the Blood of Jesus still speaks forgiveness. This son or daughter, however, must come to receive forgiveness, lest their life fall away from the living God. It is not that the Father has abandoned the son or daughter, but their sin separates them from relationship.

Never do we want to have blessings we have released be returned to sender. We want them to be able to land, but it is good to know that they are never wasted. We will talk about this some more in an upcoming chapter.

May you be blessed with understanding, revelation, insight, and clarity concerning the power of released blessings, in Jesus' name.

Chapter 18
Blessings vs. Bonds

In the prior chapter entitled "Return to Sender," Heaven[24] talked to us about the release of blessings and the landing place for those blessings being receptive. We had further questions, so we engaged Heaven again and continued our instruction.

We asked Heaven, "Can you comment about the difference between blessing someone and our revelation about the Bond Registry and requesting bonds?"

"The Bond Registry is a noted place of Heaven," was Heaven's response. "It denotes enemy activity as well as the legal means to bless and to cause an abundant blessing to offset enemy actions of negative, painful, hurtful, and constraining bonds found in that same registry. The Bond Registry revelation offsets what your enemy is legally doing because you see it recorded in

---

[24] In this engagement we were instructed on this subject but were unable to determine who exactly was instructing us.

Heaven. You come in the same legal manner to offset legal hindrances. The enemy is using ungodly bonds as a legal means against the saints by putting these bonds on the Bond Registry. The negative bond shows up in the Bond Registry against the saint, who then requests both its removal and release, as well as the placement of Godly bonds on the Registry to offset the ungodly ones. Thus, the enemy is shut down in using that method because the saints have learned how to defeat him legally, and he is upset that he has been outdone once again."

The Release of Blessing

Heaven continued, "The request of the release of a Godly bond thwarts the enemy and his demonic hordes from their activity. Isn't it just like the Father to give you two ways to do this, not just one? Do not discount one or the other, for the release of blessings and the release of Godly bonds are incredibly important.

"The enemy hopes that by using one, you will not use the other, thereby giving him an inroad in one avenue versus the other. However, when you employ both, you see the double protection, the double abundance, and the double benefit of using both tools.

Bonds have more permanency.
Blessings are more fleeting.

"I do not want to impart the impression that blessings are not important, but with the release of a blessing, it is easier for the enemy to swat it down like you would a badminton birdie. It is easier for the enemy to interfere with a spoken blessing than a bond obtained through the Courts of Heaven and placed upon one's Bond Registry. Do not get my meaning wrong here. Both are needful.

"The release of blessing is the releasing of the spoken word into the natural realm that affects the supernatural realm. When you use the spoken word to bless, you are receiving from the unseen realm (at least, this is the way it is supposed to work), by the function of the spirit, a release into the natural realm. It combines the spiritual and natural realms, but it comes through your spoken blessing and your sense of what you want to bless them with.

"With blessing, you are releasing it to the physical realm with the spoken word from the physical realm. Because it is spoken into the earth realm from the earth realm, it is easier for the enemy to swat it down. For instance, if the blessing cannot land, the enemy has a legal right to swat it down easily, and it is not able to penetrate or land on the intended subject. In a sense, it bounces back to you because it cannot land. This may be hard to understand, but the enemy has a play in this, a stake in it, or a claim to it, which is why it cannot land."

Requesting Bonds

Someone from Heaven continued the instruction, "Now, contrast that with the request to release bonds.

This is done by the believer in private, stepping into the realms of Heaven and engaging Heaven to adjudicate their justice from the realms of Heaven. It is released through the authority of the King of the Kingdom realm into the believer's life. Do you see how doing it that way circumvents the enemy in certain ways?

"The request for a bond is done from the realm of Heaven within the Courts of Heaven. You are the initiator by requesting the release of the bond from the Court of Titles and Deeds, but it is applied from the realm of Heaven. You are not releasing it into the earthly realm. Heaven is releasing it into the earth realm—because of its activity and initiation by you in the realms of Heaven, but it is done in the background. The Bond Registry is the supernatural realm affecting the natural realm."

Can You Circumvent a Blessing that Cannot Land?

We asked, "If I request a bond, does the Godly bond released by Heaven to a person's Bond Registry circumvent where a blessing may not be able to land?"

Heaven's answer was, "If you know someone in sin, and you still want to see them come into a better place from the work of the Kingdom in the background, you will need to request the release of a bond. The best bond to release is one that Holy Spirit or a messenger angel urges. Many times, when in the Court of Titles and Deeds, you can request that the angelic assistants present what

Heaven recommends you request. The bond has a better chance of productive action in the individual's life than the blessing would because the chance of the blessing being unable to land is higher. Also, you can direct the angels of the other party to be receptive to the work of the Bond Registry angels as they bring the Godly bond into that person's realm."

Heaven continued, "Do you see now that the saints are told to walk in righteousness so that blessings can land? But often, especially with those who are immature in the faith, a bond is the better thing to request because the potential recipient may be in sin or have hidden sin, and the removal of ungodly bonds with the application of Godly bonds is a two-fold whammy to offset what the individual is going through.

"Remember that with the Bond Registry, you are looking at a dual activity, removing ungodly bonds and applying Godly ones. It is not just where we appear in court to request the release of ungodly bonds that is important to remember, the additional step of requesting Godly bonds is just as important. This is the process. It is how Heaven designed it to work best."

Which to Release?

"How do you know which to release, a bond or a blessing?" we inquired.

Our heavenly instructor replied, "This would depend upon your relationship with the person," was the response. "If you are in proximity with the person (emotionally or physically) and are relatively sure the blessing can land, you will want to bless. If, however, you are dealing with a stranger, such as in Personal Advocacy Sessions, the Bond Registry is the better way to go, remembering again the twofold aspect of the Bond Registry—the removal of the ungodly bonds and the requested release of godly bonds."

Protecting Bonds and Blessings

Next, we asked, "Recently, Heaven discussed with us that during the release of a blessing from Heaven or provision from Heaven and its time of landing in the earth (or manifesting in the earth), in the time in between the release and the landing there exists a vulnerability wherein the provision needs to be protected. If Satan has a claim on a blessing because of the sin in a person's life, is there a way of safeguarding that blessing after it has been released?"

Our teacher stated, "This is the activity of the angels. This is the act of the wooing of Holy Spirit to convict that person to operate in righteousness. This is the teaching of the fathers of the faith for the continual relationship with the Godhead—Father, Son, and Holy Spirit—for maturing into all things that are righteous. These are the things that are going to affect what you are asking. The work of the enemy to steal a blessing has always been and will remain his work until his defeat. Saints are called to faith in God, hope, and knowledge of their identity, to come running back to the Father, Son, and Holy Spirit when they have drifted away. This drifting away from relationship, the relationship with the Godhead, is a lifelong quest to overcome and is sealed by the encounters the individual has with God's presence and glory of God, the miracles, the signs, and the wonders that Heaven is releasing."

Imparting Blessings

The instructor explained, "Religion cannot impart blessing. Religious traditions cannot impart blessing. Ritual cannot impart blessing. What imparts blessing is the creative function of the Word. The believer imparts out of the richness of the abundance of God into the realm of that believer that which is hoped for and that which is seen in Heaven. It is released by one to another from the increasing abundance of the seed that this causes in both realms.

"It is huge. It is much bigger than we would know, but we must begin to see it differently and to see it as the sowing of seed.

> *The sowing of blessing by word is as big as the sowing of tithes, offerings, and alms.*

"Imagine if," Heaven stated, "in the face of severe circumstances, a group of believers simply lifted their words in blessing one another; how might things change? You do not see the blessing in its immediacy because this concept is still in its infancy within the saints. As the saints mature in this understanding, they will see the manifestation of blessings more and more quickly."

"We have experienced some of that when we have the attendees at our meetings pair off and begin to bless one another,"[25] we noted.

Heaven affirmed, "When the saints share like that, if they share from the soul realm, it releases in part, but if they share from the position of having their spirit forward,[26] it is like a bomb going off. It is explosive.

"When you do that exercise, you must remind the believer to be in the spirit when releasing blessing to one who is also in the spirit. This is seismic in its impact in the earth realm. In the past, many blessed each other soul to soul, and then wondered about the timing. The soul realm is not the container of abundance—the spirit realm is.

"Just like with the request of bonds at the unction of Holy Spirit, the spirit-forward man operating in his spirit realm and blessing another individual operating from their spiritual realm releasing blessing through the first person to the second by the spoken word is a powerful act. However, if you operate in your spiritual realm from

---

[25] Described in *Cooperating with The Glory* by Dr. Ron M. Horner. LifeSpring Publishing, 2019.

[26] See "Learning to Live Spirit First" in the Appendix.

your spirit man and release a blessing, but the intended recipient is in their soul realm, they are receiving it in the wrong realm. Therefore, it leads to hope being deferred because it is not received in the right realm. If, however, they are spirit-forward when you are sowing a blessing into their spirit, and their spirit realm receives it, it is seismic. The seed of blessing germinates and grows much bigger than what you have yet seen. Receive it by your spirit," Heaven instructed.

Our instructor explained, "A way to maximize this if you can contact the person (by phone, computer, or in-person) is to say, 'I would like to release a blessing to you.' If they are receptive, both parties should call their spirit forward, instructing their soul to back up before releasing the blessing. Their part is to receive it, and they can maximize this by speaking from their heart, *'I receive this blessing imparted to me, in Jesus' name.'*"

Heaven continued, "Remember what I told you about religious traditions. Soul-realm rituals will not be the receptive soil of the word of the blessing being released, but you can receive it into your spirit man, or your spiritual realm, by your spirit. A focused, spirit-forward person releasing to a focused, spirit-forward person who actively receives it into their realm produces powerful effects.

"At the beginning of this, the soul will need to understand its secondary role in receiving this spiritual blessing of God. The spirit imparts it to the soul, but first, the spirit must receive it. You receive it with your spirit man. When you receive it with your spirit man, you must be "in the spirit" or spirit-forward, also known as being spirit receptive. Your spirit man should resonate with the connection of the other person's spirit. Here is how you know. When the other spirit-forward individual has successfully received the blessing, the receipt of it should resonate within your spirit realm, and you should feel it; you will feel the seed being sown in your spiritual realm. This is all part of being the spiritual people you are designed to be."

Kingdom Living

Our instructor explained further, "Your spirit has an identity of quantitative born-againness[27] as well as a recognition of its position in Heaven and complete acceptance of sonship. Your spirit should operate in these things with increasing revelation, knowledge, understanding, grasp, and stance. By gaining these things, your spiritual stature will increase. As it does, your spirit will translate that to your soul.

"'Keep moving in Kingdom-living, from the Kingdom that is within you,' is another way to say spirit-forward. You know how people say, 'I receive that?' What if they said, *'I welcome that spirit seed of blessing into my spirit realm. I welcome it into my realm, and I assign angels to water that in my realm.'* That is like tending the garden

---

[27] Yes, that is how our instructor said it to us.

of your spirit man with the help of angels who operate in that dimension.

"Your soul typically controls the words of your mouth, but that is not how it is meant to be. A redeemed son maturing in sonship should have his words come from his spirit.

> *If the whole church, the Bride of Christ, had all their words come from their spirit, it would change a great many things.*

A confrontation would become an edification because the flow of revelation is in the spirit. This is part of the increasing understanding and maturing of the saints. They are getting stronger in this. *We* are getting stronger in this, but we still have work to do."

The Revelation of Sonship

Our instructor explained, "The revelation of sonship is in direct correlation with the revelation of your identity as a son of God, not a son who does the work of the Father's Kingdom, but the son who is loved unconditionally by the Father.

"Remember the story of the prodigal son in scripture. We are so much more than we think we are. The Father's good pleasure is to release the Spirit of God to give courage to those willing to risk living from their spirit in this manner. A lot of humanity will miss this. This does not grieve the Father but is not the full measure of His blessing toward humanity through Christ.

Our instructor explained, "Living from the soul alone is not a sin, but neither is it the full plan of God for this generation and future generations. This is what religious tradition, religious teaching, and religiosity through ritual and tradition have tried to squelch, for these are not of the Kingdom of your Father. More and more religious tradition has blinded people from the reality of hell.

"Holy Spirit says there is a power surge coming to the earth. There is a power surge coming into the Bride. Not all will choose to walk in the power surge because many will be overwhelmed, just as a power surge short circuits the wiring in many houses. A power surge is coming to the bride to continue her growth process and display God's splendors to His chosen sons and daughters. As you have received His love and acceptance through Jesus, the Son, this power surge will sway tall buildings like a jackhammer. It will shake the ground upon which your feet walk. It will bring down ten-story buildings made by man, figuratively speaking. It will reduce the rebellious arguments of the world, the arguments of worldliness. It will set aflame a new direction in the church of Jesus Christ regarding its access to the realms of the Kingdom of God and their invitation to that realm."

Chapter 19
Surety Bonds

On the day of this engagement, Stephanie and I met with Ezekiel, the Chief Angel over the ministry. We noticed that today he looked very stoic.

He began, "Much has been accomplished. There is so much more to do."

"Is there a commissioning?" Stephanie asked.

Ezekiel said, "Remind those near the ministry to use the curtains and the veils. To utilize them. They can view it and think of it as strategy."

Stephanie replied: "Thank you, we will. We request curtains, veils, and smoke screens from the Father to use on behalf of the ministry, those near the ministry, and their families."

Stephanie exclaimed, "Immediately, I saw two huge shields come up behind Ezekiel, like wings, but they were shields."

Ezekiel said, "There is a lot of angst in the spirit. A lot of movement. It's creating a misunderstanding."

Stephanie asked, "What is a misunderstanding in the spirit regarding us?"

Ezekiel commented, "To divide, to bring misunderstanding. Misunderstanding seems small at first, but it grows within the hearts of men. Place a bond upon the people—a Surety Bond."

I asked, "What does that do, Ezekiel?"

Stephanie paused to look up the definition, "A surety bond is a contract between three parties—the **principal** (you), the **surety** (the Father), and the **obligee** (the entity requiring the bond)—in which the surety financially guarantees to an obligee that the principal will act in accordance with the terms established by the bond.[28]

"The surety provides a financial guarantee (the finished work of Jesus) to the obligee (The Father, His Kingdom dynamics) and that the principal (us) will fulfill our obligations (destiny). Therefore, a surety bond (the finished work of Jesus, the blood that gives us our inheritance) is a risk transfer mechanism. (It all falls on the guarantor, Jesus, and the finished work of the cross)."

I replied, "The bond ensures or guarantees the work gets completed, that what is promised is performed."

---

[28] https://www.suretybonds.com/what-is-a-surety-bond.html

Stephanie exclaimed, "Yes, that is so good, Heaven! Thank you."

Ezekiel continued, "The work of this ministry, the strength of it, is being felt as a ripple effect. The enemy seeks to divide."

Stephanie commented, "Ezekiel just reminded me of one of our team member's word of knowledge that he had months ago, probably November or December, where he said the Lord had impressed upon him that we, as a group, needed to continue to release the bonds of unity, the bonds of health, and the bond of safety."

Stephanie said, "I'm seeing attacks upon our team."

Ezekiel responded, "They are small attacks because there is a lot of warfare going on, but we (His commander and ranks) prevail."

Stephanie asked, "Is there anything we can request for you other than the veils and smoke screens?"

She explained the answering visual she was given, "That's a very interesting picture. He just showed me an image of himself, as Ezekiel, going to one of our team member's angels, putting his hand on that angel's right shoulder, and speaking to him as a 'brother in arms.' The message I am getting from this is that we need to remind our team members, and all that draw near to the ministry, to utilize his commanders and ranks to partner with their angels."

Stephanie said to Ezekiel, "Ezekiel, you just said there are futile attempts against the ranks."

Continuing to explain, Stephanie said, "And when he said *ranks*, I see all of us that work on behalf of the ministry and draw near. Thank you for that assurance that they are *futile* (incapable of producing any useful result: pointless) attempts against us."

Ezekiel said, "Mark my words, a thousand shall fall at your side and ten thousand at your right hand. It shall not come near you."

Stephanie replied, "That is Psalms 91:7.

"A thousand may fall at your side and ten thousand at your right hand, but it will not come near you."

"Thank you, Ezekiel. Thank You, Father, for the protection of this ministry. We praise You. We thank You, Jesus, for the way that in that, we can co-labor together with the angels."

Stephanie was reminded by Ezekiel, who spoke and said, "Call and commission us for ordered steps."

Immediately Stephanie began:

We commission you to use the veils, shields, smoke screens, and curtains, against the enemy on behalf of those who draw near to the ministry and those who work for LifeSpring and all of its components.

We commission you on behalf of this work and those who work with and draw near to it, to go with all the angels that are assigned, and to order all of our steps from the Lord.

Ezekiel, we commission you to work with each of their angels, to tell them to read their book and their scrolls to the people day and night, in Jesus' name.

Father in the name of Jesus, we ask to step into your Court of Titles and Deeds on behalf of all of those who draw near to LifeSpring Ministries, all its employees, and their families, Your Honor.

We are requesting a Surety Bond for each one of them, for each member of the Executive Leadership Team, each staff person, and their families. For those that draw near on Tuesday nights, Wednesdays, and those that watch the videos, in the name of Jesus.

We request this be released on behalf of all those mentioned to be put upon their records and all of their realms. For Ezekiel, his commanders, and ranks, to bring the surety bonds to each person, in the name of Jesus, upon their realms, their family's realms and upon their household realms.

Thank You, Your Honor.

Chapter 20
Conclusion

As we conclude this book, we must bring to your attention a word of caution we were given along with that first bond revelation. We were told:

> *Because this is new revelation,*
> *the likelihood of misuse is high.*

Human nature often seems to approach a new idea cautiously and then eventually comes to a point of embracing it. However, some don't merely embrace the idea, they run so hard with it that they set wisdom aside and swing too far in a particular direction. In the process, people get hurt, disillusioned, and more. Such is the case concerning the Courts of Heaven in the Body of Christ. What God has intended as a tool for believers has (in some cases) become a weapon—not to use against the enemy but to use against fellow believers. God is not pleased with the misuse, but that does not give us permission to release the revelation and have nothing to do with it. We must learn to use new revelation properly, with honor, and with respect.

We asked our tutor, "How can we caution them for rightful use?" His answer is, "Love is always central. Anything born out of the love of one's heart will keep you from going in the wrong direction and prevent you from having to repent for something later."

Love is indeed central. We are told that over and over throughout the Word of God.

> *Unless you love the other person,*
> *you have no right to try to seek*
> *a bond concerning them.*

That would become witchcraft, and God does not think too highly of witchcraft. Our motive must always be in their best interest.

If they are in financial need, don't you want them to have their needs met? I have been in places of financial lack before, and I can have compassion for someone in similar straits as to where I have been. From that compassion, I can rightfully request a Financial Bond on someone's behalf. The same principle applies to the other party's need. Where you have compassion and can release faith for a thing, that is what you do in the form of a bond.

May the benefits and potential of this revelation rock your world. I am requesting on your behalf a Bond of Clarity. Specifically, I request a Writ of Release of Clarity and Revelation to You Concerning the Revelation Within this Book and a Revelation of the Extravagant Love of God. May your life NEVER be the same!

———— · ————

We stepped into Heaven for some more information just before finishing the book. At the end of the session, I asked a few things about the book itself.

What do I need to add to the book?

"Pray for the people coming into understanding because of the heightened ability to use it for evil or to use it with a lot of immaturity. Write the vision and make it CLEAR. The more clearly you write, the more baby steps people can take into it.

"There are many people who desire this but often blunder their way in and then are left with a decision whether to blame God when it didn't work, or to blame you (the writer) or blame themselves. However, often the response is to blame the Lord, so your prayers out of this revelation are important and powerful."

Should I release a Bond of Clarity on behalf of those who read the book?

"That is an excellent idea, and Erik (one of our teachers) highly recommends it. He also asks if you would consider releasing a Bond of Love to the readers so they would feel granted admittance, the love of the Father through the open access to this new revelation, the availableness of it for their use, and that they would sense within it: the heart of the Father, the care of the Father, and the provision of the Father."

——— · ———

Know that in response to these instructions, I have requested both a Bond of Clarity and a Bond of Love of the Father to be released to every reader of this book. The purpose is so that you will have a real sense of the love of the Father to unveil this information to bring you to a new place of freedom and life. You will find on your Register of Bonds a Bond of Clarity and a Bond of Love listed in the left column. In the meantime, may you not merely be blessed as you read this book, but may you be bonded to clarity and to the love of the Father this day, in Jesus' name.

——— · ———

Appendix A

Bonds Listing

Godly

Ability to See

Abundance

Academia

Accelerated Healing

Accelerated Progress

Accelerated Prosperity

Acceptance

Access

Accommodation

Accountability

Accreditation

Activation

Admiration

Adoption

Adoration

Advantage

Affirmation

Affirmation

Affirmation of the Father

Affirmation of the Father and His Love

Agriculture

Anger

Anointing

Appreciation	Camaraderie
Approval	Care
Armor of God	Caring
Army of Christ	Celebration
Aroma to the Conference	Changing Mind
Association	Charity
Assurance & Security	Cheer
Authenticity of Worship	Cheerfulness
Authority	Cheerfulness & Blissfulness
Awareness	Christianity
Awareness of Presence of God	Clarity
Balance	Clarity & Discernment
Balancing of the Accounts	Clarity of Decisions
Benevolence	Clarity of Purpose
Blessing	Clarity for Studies
Blindness	Clarity of Communication
Blindness & Distorted Clarity	Clarity to Counter Disillusionment
Blissfulness	Clarity to Their Mind
Boldness	Clear Communication
Breakthrough	Clever
Brokenness	Cloaking
Business Development	Closeness

Comfort	Covenant
Commendation	Creative Writing
Commendation/Affirmation	Creativity
Communication	Creativity (not just writing)
Community	Creativity for the Authors
Compassion	Creativity in Giving
Conception	Creativity in Writing
Concern	Culture
Confidence	Dancing
Confidence in God's Goodness	Dedication / Faithfulness
Connection	Deep Sharing
Connubial Bliss	Delegation
Conscription	Delight
Consecration	Desire to Please the Lord
Construction	Desired Unity
Contentment	Destination
Control	Destiny
Convergence	Devotion
Cooperation	Diligence
Correct Understanding of Grace	Discernment
Courage	Discovery of the Hidden Riches
Courage and Calm Composure	Distraction

Divine Appointments	Excellence
Divine Exchange	Expansion
Divine Favor	Expansion
Divine Guidance	Expansion & Pioneer Spirit
Divine Project Management	Exponential Increase
Double Honor	Extravagant Love of God
Doubt	Fairness
Ease	Faith
Empathy	Faith—Experiential Faith
Empowerment	Family
Encounters	Favor & Prosperity
Encourager	Favor with FDA
Energy	Fear of the Lord
Engagement	Fear of The Lord
Engineering Mindset	Fertility
Enjoyment	Fidelity
Enlightenment	Financial Breakthrough
Enslavement	Financial Multiplication
Entrepreneurship	Financial Protection
Equity	Freedom
Estrangement	Freedom for the Nation
Evil Foreboding	Freedom Slavery

Friendship

Fruitfulness

Fruitfulness

Fulfillment

Gatekeeper (Godly)

Gathering

Generosity

Generosity/Giving

Genetics of Jesus

Gentleness

Genuineness

Gifted Future

Giftings, Anointings God

Gladness

Godly

Godly Accountability

Godly Boundaries

Godly Chronometer

Godly Curiosity

Godly Discernment

Godly Frequencies

Godly Restraint

Godly Strategy

Godly Timing

Godly Vision

Godly Wisdom

Goodness

Grace

Gratefulness

Gratefulness Toward God

Gratitude

Greater Anointing

Greater Authority

Greater Capacity for Joy

Greater Faith

Greater Intimacy

Greater Trust

Gridding/Meshing

Growth

Happiness

Healing

Healing for Adrenals

Healing/Remedy

Health

Health & Healing	Independence
Healthy Boundaries	Inheritance
Heart for the Lord	Initiative
Heavenly Frequencies	Innocence
Heavenly Strategy	Innocence/Comfort
Holiness	Integrity
Honesty	Integrity in Leaders
Honor	intercession
Honor & Respect	Intimacy
Hope	Jesus' DNA
Hopefulness	Joy
Hospitality	Joy & Laughter
Humility	Joy of the Lord
Hunger	Joy of the Lord to be their Strength
Hunger for the Things of God	Justice
Hunger for the Word of God	Keeping Track of Things
Identity	Kindness
Illegitimacy	Kingship of Jesus Christ
Illumination	Knowledge
Increase	Laughter
Increase in Demand	Leadership
Increased Love for Children	Leading Church Matters

Leaping Like a Deer	Maturity
Leverage	Maturity in One's Faith
Liberality of Thought	Memory
Liberation	Mental Clarity
Liberty	Mental Retention
Life Saving	Mental Stability
Long life	Mental Wholeness
Longevity	Mercy
Longsuffering	Miracles
Love	Multi-dimensional Learning
Love	Music
Love for One Another	Mutual Agreement
Love from Son to Mother	Nearness of God
Love of God	Nearness to God
Loyalty	Networking
Mammon	Networking (Divine Connections)
Manna	Networking/Relationship Building
Mantle	Oneness of Purpose
Mantle of Praise	Open Doors
Marital Bond	Open-mindedness
Maternal Love	Opportunity
Matrimony	Organization

Outrageous Hope	Prioritizing
Patience	Privilege
Patience with Family	Production
Patience with School Staff	Productivity
Peace	Profitability
Peace and Clarity	Profound Joy
Peaceful Sleep	Progress
Perfect Timing	Promise
Perseverance	Propriety
Persistence	Protection
Pervasiveness	Protection & Unity
Photographic Memory	Protection Around One's Heart
Physical Protection	Protection for Land
Physical Restoration	Protection of Intellectual Property
Pleasantness	Protection of Health at Cellular Level
Pleasure	Protection of Spirit
Pleasures	Protection Over the Marriage
Plenty	Prudence
Power & Might	Purity
Praise	Purity of Mind, Body, & Spirit
Precise Timing	Purposing
Presence of the Lord—Glory	Receptive Womb

- Receptivity
- Recompense
- Reconciliation
- Reconciliation to True Destiny
- Recovery
- Redemption
- Refreshing
- Regeneration
- Rejoicing
- Relational Favor
- Relational Restoration
- Release
- Release
- Release of Business/Ministry
- Release of Resources
- Relevance
- Relief
- Remedy
- Renewed Mind
- Researcher
- Respect
- Respect & Honor
- Rest
- Restitution
- Restoration
- Restoration of Destiny
- Restored Confidence
- Restored Destiny
- Restored Hope
- Restored Joy
- Restored Relationships
- Revelation
- Revelation of Father's Love
- Reward
- Righteous Godly Chronometer
- Righteousness
- Rightly Dividing the Truth
- Sacraments
- Safety
- Sales Productivity
- Salvation
- Security
- Seeing into the Spirit
- Self-acceptance

Self-confidence	Strategy
Self-effort	Strength
Self-preservation	Strengthened Maternal Love
Self-worth	Strong Self-worth
Serendipity	Studiousness
Severing	Success
Shalom	Success in All Endeavors
Sharing	Supernatural Miracles
Shield of Faith	Supernatural Provisions
Sleep & Rest	Support
Social Justice	Sweetness
Sonship	Sympathy
Sound Mind	Synchronized Favor
Sound Mind & Insights	Teacher of the Faith
Soundness of Mind	Teamwork
Sowing & Reaping	Telemetry
Special Solutions	Tenaciousness
Spiritual Sight	Tenacity
Stability	Time Redemption
Steadfastness	Total Consecration
Storytelling	Tranquility
Strategizing	Transparency

Travel	Unity of All
Treasures	Unsearchable Riches
Tribute	Unveiling
True Discernment	Vengeance
True Identity	Victory
True Trinity	Vision
Trust	Voice to be Heard
Trusting in God	Walking in my Destiny
Truth	Wealth Creation, Generosity
Truthfulness	Whistling
Uncloaking	Wholeness
Understanding	Wholeness (Immune System)
Understanding of Their Purpose	Wholeness in Physical Health
Understanding The Power of Community	Wholeness in Mental Health
	Wholeness of Soul
Understanding the Power of Prayer	Windfall
	Wisdom
Understanding with Family	Wisdom for the Marriage
Understanding w/School Staff	Wonder
Union	Worship
Unity	Worshipping in Spirit & Truth
Unity for the Family	Worthiness
Unity in Place	

Ungodly Bonds

Abandonment

Abomination

Accreditation

Accusation

Addiction

Adultery

Adversity

Affliction

Alienation

Alienation or Estrangement

Alienation/Estrangement

Allegiance to Rah

An Ungodly Chronometer

Anger

Anger & Rage

Anguish

Annihilation

Anxiety

Anxiety

Attack

Backbiting

Backstabbing

Backwardness

Bankruptcy

Betrayal

Bitterness (emotional)

Bleeding

Blindness

Bondage

Broken heartedness -

Calamity

Calcification

Catastrophe

Catholicism

Celestial Slavery	Cunning & Trickery
Chaos	Deafness
Chaos/Confusion	Death
Cheating	Death & Destruction
Cloak of Invisibility	Death on the Generations
Cloaking	Debauchery
Cloaking	Deceit
Co-dependency	Deception
Combativeness	Deception
Comfort Over Calling	Defamation
Competition	Defamation
Condemnation	Defamation of Character
Condescension	Defaming
Confusion	Defeat
Contempt	Deferment
Control	Defilement
Corruption	Degeneration
Coy	Degradation
Criticism/Judging	Delay
Cruelty	Denial
Culture	Depravity
Cunning	Depression

Deprivation
Derision
Derision Toward God
Derision Toward Man
Desecration
Despair
Despair—Family
Desperation
Despondent
Destruction
Destruction: Mental/Financial
Destruction of Relationships
Detachment
Detainment on Ministry
Determent
Deterrence
Deterrent
Detriment
Detriment or Loss
Detriment & Loss
Deviation of Grace
Difficulty

Diminished Returns
Disassociation
Disconnection
Discord
Disengagement
Disgruntlement
Dishonest Scales
Dishonor
Dislocation
Dismemberment
Displacement
Dissatisfaction
Disillusionment
Dissociation
Dissociation/Separation
Distance
Distortion
Disunity
Disunity in the Marriage
Divination
Divination (False Light)
Division

- Divisiveness
- Divisiveness & Strife
- Double Mindedness
- Doubt
- Doubting
- Dread
- Dread/Evil Foreboding
- Drudgery
- Enmity
- Enslavement
- Entanglement
- Entrapment
- Envy
- Estrangement
- Evasiveness
- Evil foreboding
- Failure
- False Armor
- False Responsibility
- Fascination
- Fear
- Fear of Being Deceived
- Fear of failure
- Fear of Man
- Fear of Success
- Feeling Like an Orphan
- Food Addictions
- Forlorn
- Fornication
- Frustration
- Galactic Troubles
- Galactic Devices
- Galactical Substances
- Gatekeeper (Opposite of a Protector)
- Getting Attacked
- Greed
- Grief
- Guilt
- Harassment
- Hardness of Heart
- Hardship
- Harm
- Hate

Hatred	Injustice
Held Back	Insecurity
Hesitation	Insignificance & Feeling Small
Hiraeth	Insomnia
Hindrance	Instability
Hope Deferred	Intellectualism
Hopelessness	Interference in Communication
Hope lost	Intimidation
Humanism	Intimidation/Control
Hypocrisy	Intimidation/Hesitation
Idolatry	Invisibility
Illusion	Isolation
Immaturity	Jealousy
Impatience	Jeopardy
Impeding Judgment	Judgment
Indignation	King of the Mountain
Infirmities	Lack
Infirmity	Leviathan
Inflammation	Lies
Inflammations	Loss
Inheritance	Loss of Confidence in God's Power
Iniquity	Loyalty

Malfunction	Ovation
Maligning	Overshadowing
Manipulation	Paganism
Masking	Pain
Mental Sabotage	Pain (Emotional)
Misery	Painful Progress (Drudgery)
Mockery	Panic
Mockery of God	Persecution
Mocking	Persecution/Accusation
Murder	Perversion
Murmuring	Pharisaism
Murmuring Against God	Pleasures
Murmuring/Complaining	Pollution
Neediness	Prejudice
Neglect	Premature Death
No Love	Prickliness
No Relief	Pride
Non-acceptance	Procrastination
Not Having Accountability	Profane Worship
Obliviousness	Rage
Obsession	Rebellion
Orphanhood	Regret

Rejection	Self-hatred
Religiosity	Self-imprisonment
Relinquishment	Self-preservation
Repeated Debt	Self-righteousness
Resistance	Separation
Restraint	Separateness
Retaliation	Severing
Rewind	Shame
Rivalry	Shearing
Sabotage	Sin
Sadness or Forlorn	Slander
Santeria (Witchcraft)	Slavery
Sarcasm	Slow Start
Scarring	Sorcery
Scattering	Sorcery/Witchcraft
Seclusion	Sorrow
Seething Fury	Spear
Self-aggrandizement	Spirit of Fear
Self-defamation	Stagnation
Self-destruction	Stifling/Muzzling
Self-effort	Strategic Attack
Self-exaltation	Strife

Strife (Woman to Woman)
Striving
Striving & Self-Effort
Suicide
Suspicion
Synchronized Chaos
Synchronized Destruction
Tenacity
Terror
Thanklessness
Theft
Thievery
Time Repression
Torment
Tormenting
Torture
Tracking
Tragedy
Transference
Trauma
Trauma & Fear
Trauma to Time

Treachery
Trepidation
Tribology
Trickery
Triggering
Trilogy
Tug-of-wars
Unbalanced Scales
Unbelief
Uncertainty
Unconcern
Ungodly Boundaries
Ungodly Chronometer
Ungodly Leaders
Ungodly Propriety
Ungodly Treasury
Ungratefulness
Unhealthy Genetics
Unhealthy Relationships
Unholy Betrothal
Unholy Grief
Unjust Scales

Unrighteous Chronometer

Unsettledness

Usury

Voodoo

Waywardness

Weakness

Wicked Illumination

Wicked Schemes

Witchcraft

Withholding from Need

Worry

Yoke of Sadness

Works Cited

American Heritage Dictionary of the English Language, Fifth Edition. Houghton Mifflin Harcourt Publishing Company, 2016.

chat.opentai.com/chat. 23 08 2023. <chat.opentai.com/chat>.

Oxford Dictionary: Bond. n.d. <https://www.lexico.com/en/definition/bond>.

Unknown. *Freedictionary.com/banz.* 5 January 2019. <https://www.thefreedictionary.com/Bann>.

Description

Have you experienced a situation where nothing seemed to move it? Often something has been hidden from us, keeping us trapped. From the realms of Heaven, revelation has been released to bring individuals, and groups of people including cities, even nations to new levels of freedom through the power of bonds.

Bonds are powerful ways to release the might and power of God, clarity, peace, wisdom, and so much more into situations to effect change. Bonds are beautiful free things that Heaven wants us to utilize more because they affect things swiftly and because of the ease at which change can come. This revelation could not have been timelier! It will propel the church to release bonds of life-giving power into the earth and see lasting change.

——— · ———

About the Author

Dr. Ron Horner is an apostolic teacher specializing in the Courts of Heaven. He has written over twenty books on the Courts of Heaven, Engaging Heaven, working with angels, and living from revelation.

He currently trains people in engaging the Courts of Heaven in a weekly online teaching session. You can register to participate and discover more about the Courts of Heaven prayer paradigm on his various websites, classes, products, and services found here:

www.ronhorner.com

Other Books by Dr. Ron M. Horner

Building Your Business from Heaven Down

Building Your Business from Heaven Down 2.0

Building Your Business with the Blueprint of Heaven

Commissioning Angels – Volume 1

Cooperating with The Glory

Courts of Heaven Process Charts

Dealing with Trusts & Consequential Liens from the Courts of Heaven

Engaging Angels in the Realms of Heaven

Engaging Heaven for Revelation – Volume 1

Engaging Heaven for Revelation – Volume 2

Engaging Heaven for Trade

Engaging the Courts for Ownership & Order

Engaging the Courts for Your City (*Paperback, Leader's Guide & Workbook*)

Engaging the Courts of Healing & the Healing Garden

Engaging the Courts of Heaven

Engaging the Help Desk of the Courts of Heaven

Engaging the Mercy Court of Heaven

Four Keys to Dismantling Accusations

Freedom from Mithraism

Kingdom Dynamics – Volume 1

Kingdom Dynamics – Volume 2

Let's Get it Right!

Lingering Human Spirits

Lingering Human Spirits – Volume 2

Living Spirit Forward

Overcoming the False Verdicts of Freemasonry

Overcoming Verdicts from the Courts of Hell

Releasing Bonds from the Courts of Heaven

Unlocking Spiritual Seeing

SPANISH

Cómo Proceder en la Corte Celestial de Misericordia

Las Cuatro Llaves para Anular las Acusaciones

Liberando Bonos en las Cortes Celestiales

Liberando Su Visión Espiritual

Sea Libre del Mitraísmo

Tablas de Proceso de la Cortes del Cielo

Viviendo desde el Espíritu

www.ingramcontent.com/pod-product-compliance
Lightning Source LLC
Chambersburg PA
CBHW032249150426
43195CB00008BA/385